William Webbe

A Discourse of English Poetrie

1586

William Webbe

A Discourse of English Poetrie
1586

ISBN/EAN: 9783337817350

Printed in Europe, USA, Canada, Australia, Japan

Cover: Foto ©Thomas Meinert / pixelio.de

More available books at **www.hansebooks.com**

English Reprints

WILLIAM WEBBE

Graduate

A Discourse of English Poetrie

1586

EDITED BY

E D W A R D   A R B E R

F.S.A. ETC. LATE EXAMINER IN ENGLISH
LANGUAGE AND LITERATURE
TO THE UNIVERSITY OF
LONDON

WESTMINSTER

A. CONSTABLE AND CO.

1895

CONTENTS

NOTES

of

WILLIAM WEBBE.

* Probable or approximate dates.

Very little is known of the Author of this work. The suggestion that he was the William Webbe, M.A., one of the joint Authors of a topographical book *The Vale Royal*, 1648, fol., is quite anachronistic.

Messrs. Cooper, in *Athenæ Cantabrigiensis, ii.* 12. *Ed.* 1861, state that our Author "was a graduate of this University, but we have no means of determining his college. One of this name, who was of St. John's College, was B.A. 1572-3 [the same year as Spenser], as was another who was of Catharine Hall in 1581-2. His place of residence is unknown, although it may perhaps be inferred that it was in or near the county of Suffolk. We have no information as to his position in life, or the time or place of his death. He was evidently a man of superior intellect and no mean attainments." [Our Author apparently witnessed *Tancred and Gismund* in 1568, and being evidently acquainted with Gabriel Harvey and Spenser (who left Cambridge in 1578), must be the earlier graduate of the above two Webbes.]

1568.	*Tancred and Gismund*, written by five members of the Inner Temple, the first letters of whose names are attached to the several acts, viz., Rod. Staff; Hen. No[well?]; G. All; Ch. Hat[ton?]; and R. W[ilmot] : is 'curiously acted in view of her Maiesty, by whom it was then princely accepted.'

Webbe appears to have been present at the representation : see **1591.** Mr. J. P. Collier in his edition of 'Dodsley's *Old Plays*,' i. 153, prints from a MS. what is apparently a portion of this Tragedy as it was then acted, written in alternate rhymes. He also states in his *Hist. of Dram. Poet.* that it ' is the earliest English play extant, the plot of which is known to be derived from an Italian novel," *iii.* 13. *Ed.* 1831.

*1572-3.	Our Author takes his B.A. at Cambridge.
1582. Nov. 28.	Gabriel Poyntz presented Robert Wilmott, clerk to the Rectory of North Okendon, Essex : 18 miles from London. *Newcourt Repertorium, ii.* 447. *Ed.* 1710.

Flemyngs is a large manor house in Essex in the parish of Runwell, in the hundred of Chelmsford ; from which town it is ten miles distant, and about twenty-nine miles from London. 'This house commands extensive views of some parts of the county and of Kent, including more than thirty parish churches.'

Edward Sulyard succeeded, on the death of his father Eustace in 1546, to Flemyngs and other possessions. He had two sons, Edward and Thomas, and a daughter named Elizabeth. He was knighted on 23 July 1603 at Whitehall by James I, before his coronation : and died in June 1610. Of his two sons, Edward died without issue; Thomas, *b.* 1573, was knighted, and *d.* March 1634; leaving a son Edward, who *d.* 7 Nov. 1692 without issue, ' the last of the house and family.' See *W. Berry, County Gen. Essex*, 64. T. Wright, *Hist. of Essex, i.* 142, 143. *Ed.* 1831. J. P[hilipot] *Knts. Batch. made by James I.* 1660.

*1583 or 4.	Webbe appears to have been at this time private tutor to Mr. Sulyard's two sons, for he presented his MS. translation (now lost) of the *Georgics* to Mr. Sulyard : see *pp.* 55 and 16.
1585. Dec. 2.	The Dean and Chapter of St. Paul's appoint Robert Wilmott, M.A., to the Vicarage of Horndon on the Hill, twenty-four miles from London, and a few miles from Flemyngs, where his friend Webbe was a private tutor. *Newcourt, idem. ii.* 343.

1586.   Of ' the pregnant ympes of right excellent hope,' Thomas
Sulyard was about thirteen years old, and his brother Edward
was older than him.
W. Webbe writes the present work in the summer evenings.

Sept. 4. It is thus registered for publication.

"Robt. Walley
John Charlewood, Rd. of them, for printinge A Discourse oı
englishe poetrye . . . . vjᵈ."
J. P. Collier, Extr. of Stat. Co.'s Regrs. ii., 215. *Ed.* 1849.

1587. Feb. 5. Margaret, the mother of Mr. Sulyard died. She is buried at
Runwell.

1588.   Warton quotes "a small black-lettered tract entitled *The
Touch-stone of Wittes,* chiefly compiled, with some slender
additions, from William Webbe's *Discourse of English
Poetrie,* written by Edward Hake, and printed at London by
Edmund Bollifant." *p.* 804. *Ed.* 1870.

Our Author—his pupils growing to manhood—then appears to have gone,
possibly also in the same capacity of private tutor into the family of Henry
Grey, Esquire [created Baron Grey of Groby, 21 July 1603 : *d.* 1614] at
Pirgo, in the parish of Havering atte Bower, Essex ; fifteen miles from Lon-
don.   Dugdale states that the first husband of one of the daughters of this
Henry Grey, Esquire, was a *William Sulyard,* Esquire.   *Baron.* i. 722.
Ed. 1675. From this old Palace of the Queens of England Webbe wrote the fol-
lowing letter to Wilmott, which is reprinted in the revised edition of *Tan-
cred and Gismund* published in 1592: of which there are copies in the
Bodleian, and at Bridgewater House, and an imperfect one in the British
Museum (C. 34, e. 44).

1591. Aug. 8.   *To his frend R. W.* Master *R. VV.* looke not now for
the tearmes of an intreator, I wil beg no longer, and for your
promises, I wil refuse them as bad paiment : neither can I be
satisfied with any thing, but a peremptorie performance of an
old intention of yours, the publishing I meane of those wast
papers (as it pleaseth you to cal them, but as I esteem them,
a most exquisite inuention) of *Gismunds* Tragedie. Thinke
not to shift me off with longer delayes, nor alledge more ex-
cuses to get further respite, least I arrest you with my *Actum
est,* and commence such a Sute of vnkindenesse against you,
as when the case shall be scand before the Iudges of courtesie,
the court will crie out of your immoderat modestie. And thus
much I tel you before, you shal not be able to wage against
me in the charges growing vpon this action, especially, if the
worshipful company of the Inner temple gentlemen patronize
my cause, as vndoubtedly they wil, yea, and rather plead
partially for me then let my cause miscary, because them-
selues are parties. The tragedie was by them most pithely
framed, and no lesse curiously acted in view of her Maiesty,
by whom it was then as princely accepted, as of the whole
honorable audience notably applauded : yea, and of al men
generally desired, as a work, either in statelines of shew,
depth of conceit, or true ornaments of poeticall arte, inferior
to none of the best in that kinde : no, were the Roman *Seneca*
the censurer. The braue youths that then (to their high
praises) so feelingly performed the same in action, did shortly
after lay vp the booke vnregarded, or perhaps let it run
abroade (as many parentes doe their children once past
dandling) not respecting so much what hard fortune might
befall it being out of their fingers, as how their heroical wits
might againe be quickly conceiued with new inuentions of
like worthines, wherof they haue been euer since wonderfull
fertill.   But this orphan of theirs (for he wandreth as it were
fatherlesse,) hath notwithstanding, by the rare and bewtiful
perfections appearing in him, betherto neuer wanted great

fauourers, and louing preseruers. Among whom I cannot sufficiently commend your more then charitable zeale, and scholerly compassion towards him, that haue not only rescued and defended him from the deuouring iawes of obliuion, but vouchsafed also to apparrel him in a new sute at your own charges, wherein he may again more boldly come abroad, and by your permission returne to his olde parents, clothed perhaps not in richer or more costly furniture than it went from them, but in handsomnes and fashion more answerable to these times, wherein fashions are so often altered. Let one word suffice for your encouragement herein: namely, your commendable pains in disrobing him of his antike curiositie, and adorning him with the approoued guise of our stateliest Englishe termes (not diminishing, but augmenting his artificiall colours of absolute poesie, deriued from his first parents) cannot but bee grateful to most mens appetites, who vpon our experience we know highly to esteem such lofty measures of sententiously composed Tragedies.

How much you shal make me, and the rest of your priuate frends beholding vnto you, I list not to discourse: and therefore grounding vpon these alledged reasons, that the suppressing of this Tragedie, so worthy for ye presse, were no other thing then wilfully to defraud your selfe of an vniuersall thank, your frends of their expectations, and sweete G. of a famous eternitie. I will cease to doubt of any other pretence to cloake your bashfulnesse, hoping to read it in print (which lately lay neglected amongst your papers) at our next appointed meeting.

I bid you heartely farewell. From Pyrgo in Essex, August the eight, 1591. *Tuus fide et facultate.* GUIL. WEBBE.

It may also be noted that Wilmott dedicated this revised tragedy to two Essex ladies: one of whom was Lady Anne Grey, the daughter of Lord Windsor, and the wife of the above-mentioned Henry Grey, Esquire of Pirgo.

That the above R. Wilmott, Clergyman, is the same as the Reviser of the play appears from the following passage in his Preface.

"Hereupon I have indured some conflicts between reason and judgement, whether it were convenient for the commonwealth. and the *indecorum* of my calling (as some think it) that the memory of *Tancred's* Tragedy should be again by my means revised, which the oftner I read over, and the more I considered thereon, the sooner I was won to consent thereunto: calling to mind that neither the thrice reverend and learned father, M. Beza, was ashamed in his younger years to send abroad, in his own name, his Tragedy of *Abraham*, nor that rare Scot (the scholar of our age) *Buchanan*, his most pathetical *Ieptha.*" '*Dodsley's Old Plays.' ii.* 165. Ed. by J. P. Collier, 1825.

If the identity may be considered as established, Wilmott the Poet lived on till 1619: when he was succeeded on his death by W. Jackson, in the Rectory of North Okendon. *Newcourt, idem. ii.* 447.

No later information concerning W. Webbe than the above letter, has yet been recovered.

CONTEMPORARY ENGLISH AUTHORS
REFERRED TO IN THE FOLLOWING *Difcourfe.*

THE TRANSLATORS.

SENECA.

OVID.

VIRGIL.

A Difcourfe of Englifh Poetrie

INTRODUCTION.

Part from the exceffive rarity of this work, two copies of it only being known; it deferves permanent republication as a good example of the beft form of Effay Writing of its time; and as one of the feries of Poetical Criticifms before the advent of Shakefpeare as a writer, the ftudy of which is fo effential to a right underftanding of our beft Verfe.

Although Poetry is the moft ethereal part of Thought and Expreffion; though Poets muft be born and cannot be made: yet is there an art of Poefy; fet forth long ago by Horace but varying with differing languages and countries, and even with different ages in the life of the fame country. In our tongue—Milton only excepted—there is nothing approaching, either in the average merit of the Journeymen or the fuperlative excellence of the few Mafter-Craftfmen, the Poefy of the Elizabethan age. Hence the value of thefe early Poetical Criticifms. Their difcuffion of principles is moft helpful to all readers in the difcernment of the fubtle beauties of the numberlefs poems of that era: while for thofe who can, and who will; they will be found fingularly fuggeftive in the training of their own Power of Song, for the inftruction and delight of this and future generations.

A Cambridge graduate; the private tutor, for fome two or three years paft, to Edward and Thomas Sul-

yard, the fons of Edward Sulyard Efquire, of Flemyngs, fituated in Effex, fome thirty miles diftant from
London. our Author gave his leifure hours to the
ftudy of Latin and Englifh poetry.

He had acquainted himfelf with our older Poets,
and with the contemporary verfe: and, thinking for
himfelf, he endeavoured to fee exactly what Englifh
poetry actually was, and what it might and fhould become. Doubtlefs in his walks in the large park fur-
rounding the Old Manor Houfe this fubject often occupied his thoughts, and he fat down to commit his
opinions to the prefs, in the prefence and quietude of
a large and fair landfcape ftretching far away fouth-
ward beyond the Thames into Kent, diverfified with
the fpires of many churches and the mafts of many
paffing fhips : and all illuminated with the glow and
glory of the fummer evenings of 1586.

Webbe was as much affected with the ' immoderate
modefty' with which, five years later, he charged Wil-
mot, as any of the writers of that age. He dreads, at
p. 55, the unauthorized publication of his verfion of
the *Georgics*, and he muft have been moved deeply
by 'the rude multitude of rufticall Rymers, who will
be called Poets' before he ventured to advocate in
print 'the reformation of our Englifh Verfe,' *i.e.*, the
abandonment of Rhyme for Metre.

He calls his work 'a fleight fomewhat compyled for
recreation, in the intermyffions of my daylie bufineffe,'
yet it is the moft extenfive piece of Poetical Criticifm
that had hitherto appeared. He had read, for he
quotes at *p.* 64, G. Gafcoigne's *Certayne Notes, &c.*,
1575: alfo *Three proper and wittie, familiar Letters*,
by Immerito [Edmund Spenfer] and G[abriel H[arvey]
1580, to which he alludes at *p.* 36. He may have
heard of Sir P. Sidney's *Apologie for Poetrie* [1582],
then circulating in manufcript, or of the young Scotch
King's *Reulis and Cautelis of Scottifh Poefie*, then being

publiſhed at Edinburgh. Yet none of theſe is ſo
lengthy, nor deals with the ſame extent of ſubjeĉt,
nor is illuſtrated by original examples, as is this
Diſcourſe.

Though the book is an honeſt one, faithfully repre-
ſenting the author's robuſt mind; it was written under
the ſtrong influence of three works: Aſcham's *Schole-
maſter*, 1570; Edwardes' *Paradiſe of Dainty Deviſes*,
1576; and Spenſer's *Shepherdes Calender*, anonymouſly
publiſhed, without the author's conſent, by E. K. [*i.e.,*
Edward Kirke, as is generally believed] in 1579. He
follows Aſcham as to the origin of Rhyme; and alſo in
his error as to Simmias Rhodias at *p.* 57, &c. He quotes
W. Hunnis' poem at *p.* 66, from the collection of
Edwardes. It is alſo Webbe's great merit as a lover
and judge of poetry, that he inſtinctively fixes upon
the *Shepherdes Calender* (never openly acknowledged
by Spenſer in his lifetime) as the revelation of a great
poet, as great an Engliſh Poet indeed, as had yet appeared. That Paſtoral Poem gave Webbe a higher
reverence for Spenſer than his great Allegory breeds
reſpect for him in many, now-a-days.

The facility of Rhyme, at a time when there were many
wonderfully facile Rhymers, induced Aſcham, Webbe,
and many others to ſeek after a more difficult form of
Engliſh verſe. Claſſical feet Webbe himſelf experi-
enced to be a 'troubleſome and vnpleaſant peece of
labour,' ſo he ſought after ſomething more adapted to
the nature of the language, 'ſome perfect platforme or
Proſodia of verſifying.' Blank verſe would have ſatiſ-
fied him, but he did not recogniſe its merits in Surrey's
tranſlation of the *Æneid.* He is, however, warm in
his praiſe of Phaer's verſion of that work in hexameters: and gives us three pieces of reformed verſe of
his own coinage; two in hexameters, and one in
ſapphics.

Finally, Webbe wrote 'theſe fewe leaues' 'to ſtirre

vppe some other of meete abilitie, to bestowe trauell in this matter.' His wish had been anticipated. Already a Master Critic was at work—we know not for certainty whether it was George Puttenham, or who else—who, beginning to write in 1585, published in 1589 *The Arte of English Poesie* : which is the largest and ablest criticism of English Poesy that appeared in print, during the reign of Elizabeth.

BIBLIOGRAPHY.

Issues in the Author's lifetime.

I.—*As a separate publication.*

1. 1586. London. 1 vol. 4to. See title on opposite page.

> Of the two copies known, the one here reprinted is among the Malone books in the Bodleian. The other passed from hand to hand at the following sales : always increasing in price.
>
> 1773. APR. 8. Mr. West's sale, No. 1856, 10s. 6d., to Mr. Pearson.
> 1778. APR. 22. Mr. Pearson's sale, No. 1888, £3, 5s., to Mr. Stevens.
> 1800. MAY 19. Mr Stevens' sale, No. 1128, £8, 8s., to the Duke of Roxburghe.
> 1812. JUNE 2. The Roxburghe sale, No. 3168, £64, to the Marquis of Blandford.

Issues since the Author's death.

I.—*As a separate publication.*

3. 1870. DEC. 1. London. *English Reprints* : see title at 1 vol. 8vo. *p.* 1.

II.— *With other works.*

2. 1815. London. *Ancient Critical Essays.* Ed. by J. Haslewood. *A Discourse of English Poetrie* occupies Vol. ii., *pp.* 13-95. 2 vols. 4to.

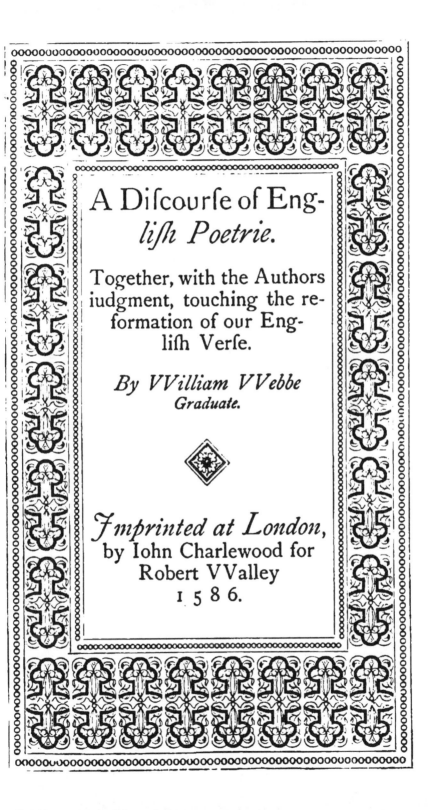

A Difcourse of Eng-
lifh Poetrie.

Together, with the Authors
iudgment, touching the reformation of our Eng-
lifh Verfe.

By VVilliam VVebbe
Graduate.

Imprinted at London,
by Iohn Charlewood for
Robert VValley
1 5 8 6.

To the right vvorſhip=

full, learned, and moſt gentle Gentleman, *my verie good Master, Ma.*
Edward Suliard, Eſquire. VV. VV.
wyſheth his harts deſire.

(∴)

Ay it pleaſe you Syr, *thys once*
more to beare with my rudenes, in
preſenting vnto your viewe, an other
ſlender conceite, of my ſimple capa-
city: wherin although I am not able
to bring you anie thing, which is
meete to detaine you from your more ſerious matters:
yet vppon my knowledge of your former courteſy and
your fauourable countenaunce towardes all enterpriſes
of Learning, I dare make bold to craue your accustomed
patience, in turning ouer ſome of theſe fewe leaues, which
I ſhall account a greater recompence, then the wryting
thereof may deſerue.

The firme hope of your wonted gentlenes, not any good lyking of myne owne labour, made me thus preſumptuouſly to craue your worships patronage for my poore booke. A pretty aunſwere is reported by ſome to be made by Appelles *to King* Alexander, *who (in diſport) taking vp one of his penſilles to drawe a line, and asking the Paynters iudgment of his draught,* It is doone *(quoth Apelles)* like a King: *meaning indeede it was drawen as he pleaſed, but was nothing leſſe then good workmanshippe. My ſelfe in like ſort, taking vppon me, to make a draught of* Engliſh Poetry, *and requeſting your worſhyps cenſure of the ſame, you wyll perhaps gyue me thys verdict,* It was doone like a Scholler, *meaning, as I could, but indeede more like to a learner, then one through grounded in Poeticall workmanship.*

Alexander *in drawing his lyne, leaned ſometime too hard, otherwhyle too ſoft, as neuer hauing beene apprentice to the Arte: I in drawing this Poeticall diſcourſe, make it ſome where to ſtraight (leauing out the cheeſe colloures and ornaments of Poetry) in an other place to wyde (ſtuffing in peeces little pertinent to true Poetry) as one neuer acquainted wyth the learned Muſes. What then? as he being a king, myght meddle in what Scyence him liſted, though therein hee had no skyll: ſo I beeing a learner, wyll trye my cunning in ſome parts of Learning, though neuer ſo ſimple.*

Nowe, as for my ſaucie preſſing vppon your expected fauor in crauing your iudgment, I beſeech you let me

*make thys excuſe: that whereas true Gentilitie did
neuer withdrawe her louing affection from Lady Learning, so I am perſwaded, that your worshyppe cannot
chuſe, but continue your wonted fauourable benignitie
towardes all the indeuourers to learning, of which
corporation I doo indeede profeſſe my ſelfe one ſillie
member.*

*For ſith the wryters of all ages, haue ſought as an vn-
doubted Bulwarke and stedfaſt ſauegarde the patronage
of Nobilitye, (a ſhielde as ſure as can be to learning)
wherin to ſhrowde and ſafelye place their ſeuerall inuentions: why should not I ſeeke ſome harbour for' my poore
trauell to reste and ſtaye vppon, beeing of it ſelfe vnable
to ſhyft the carping cauilles and byting ſcornes of lewde
controllers ?*

*And in trueth, where myght I rather chooſe a ſure
defence and readye refuge for the ſame, then where I ſee
perfecte Gentilitye, and nobleneſſe of minde, to be faſte
lyncked with excellencie of learning and affable courteſye?
Moreouer, adde thys to the ende of myne excuſe: that I
ſende it into your ſight, not as anie wyttie peece of worke
that may delight you: but being a ſleight ſomewhat compyled for recreation, in the intermyſſions of my daylie
buſineſſe, (euen thys Summer Eueninges) as a token of
that earnest and vnquenchable deſyre I haue to shewe my
ſelfe duetifull and welwylling towardes you. VVherevnto
I am continually enflamed more and more, when I con-
ſider eyther your fauourable freendshyppe vſed towardes*

my ſelfe, or your gentle countenaunce ſhewed to my ſimple trauelles. The one I haue tryed in that homely tranſla-tion I preſented vnto you: the other I finde true in your curteous putting to my truſt, and dooing me ſo great honeſty and credite, with the charge of theſe toward young Gentlemen your ſonnes.

To which pregnant ympes of right excellent hope, I would I were able, or you myght haue occaſion to make triall of my louing minde: who ſhoulde well perceyue my ſelfe to remayne vnto them a faythfull and truſty Achates, euen ſo farre as my wealth my woe, my power or perrill, my penne or witte, my health or lyfe may ſerue to ſerche myne ability.

Huge heapes of wordes I myght pyle together to trouble you withall: eyther of my ſelfe or of my dooinges, (as ſome doo) or of your worſhyppes commendable vertues (as the moſte doo) But I purpoſely chuſe rather to let paſſe the ſpreading of that worthy fame which you haue euer deſerued, then to runne in ſuſpicion of fawning flattery which I euer abhorred.

Therefore once againe crauing your gentle pardon, and patience in your ouerlooking thys rude Epiſtle: and wyſhing more happineſſe then my penne can expreſſe to you and your whole retinewe, I rest.

(∴)

Your worſhippes faithfull
Seruant. VV. VV.

A Preface to the noble *Poets of Englande.*

Mong the innumerable fortes of Eng-
lyfhe Bookes, and infinite fardles of
printed pamphlets, wherewith thys
Countrey is peftered, all fhoppes
ftuffed, and euery ftudy furnifhed:
the greateft part I thinke in any
one kinde, are fuch as are either
meere Poeticall, or which tende in fome refpecte (as
either in matter or forme) to Poetry. Of fuch Bookes
therfore, fith I haue beene one, that haue had a
defire to reade not the feweft, and becaufe it is an
argument, which men of great learning haue no ley-
fure to handle, or at leaft hauing to doo with more
ferious matters doo leaft regarde: If I write fomething,
concerning what I thinke of our Englifh Poets, or aduenture to fette downe my fimple iudgement of Englifh
Poetrie, I truft the learned Poets will giue me leaue,
and vouchfafe my Booke paffage, as beeing for the
rudeneffe thereof no preiudice to their noble ftudies,
but euen (as my intent is) an *inftar cotis* to ftirre vppe
fome other of meete abilitie, to beftowe trauell in this
matter: whereby I thinke wee may not onelie get the
meanes which wee yet want, to difcerne betweene good
writers and badde, but perhappes alfo challenge from
the rude multitude of rufticall Rymers, who will be
called Poets, the right practife and orderly courfe of
true Poetry.

It is to be wondred at of all, and is lamented of

manie, that where as all kinde of good learning, haue
afpyred to royall dignitie and ftatelie grace in our
Englifh tongue, being not onelie founded, defended,
maintained, and enlarged, but alfo purged from faultes,
weeded of errours, and pollifhed from barbaroufnes, by
men of great authoritie and iudgement: onelie Poetrie
hath founde feweft frends to amende it, thofe that can,
referuing theyr fkyll to themfelues, thofe that cannot,
running headlong vppon it, thinking to garnifh it with
their deuifes, but more corrupting it with fantafticall
errours.　VVhat fhoulde be the caufe, that our Englifh
fpeeche in fome of the wyfeft mens iudgements, hath
neuer attained to anie fufficient ripenes, nay not ful
auoided the reproch of barbaroufnes in Poetry? the
rudenes of the Countrey, or bafeneffe of wytts: or the
courfe *Dialect* of the fpeeche? experience vtterlie dif-
proueth it to be anie of thefe: what then? furelie the
canckred enmitie of curious cuftome: which as it neuer
was great freend to any good learning, fo in this hath
it grounded in the moft, fuch a negligent perfwafion
of an impoffibilitie in matching the beft, that the fineft
witts and moft diuine heades, haue contented themfelues with a bafe kinde of fingering: rather debafing
theyr faculties, in fetting forth theyr fkyll in the cour-
feft manner, then for breaking cuftome, they would
labour to adorne their Countrey and aduaunce their
ftyle with the higheft and moft learnedft toppe of
true Poetry.　The rudenes or vnaptneffe of our
Countrey to be either none or no hinderaunce, if
reformation were made accordinglie, the exquifite excellency in all kindes of good learning nowe flourifh-
ing among vs, inferiour to none other nation, may
fufficiently declare.

That there be as ſharpe and quicke wittes in England as euer were among the peereleſſe Grecians, or
renowmed Romaines, it were a note of no witte at all
in me to deny. And is our ſpeeche ſo courſe, or our
phraſe ſo harſhe, that Poetry cannot therein finde a
vayne whereby it may appeare like it ſelfe? why ſhould
we think ſo baſely of this? rather then of her ſiſter, I
meane Rhetoricall *Eloquution,* which as they were by
byrth Twyns, by kinde the ſame, by originall of one
deſcent: ſo no doubt, as Eloquence hath founde ſuch
fauoures, in the Engliſh tongue, as ſhe frequenteth not
any more gladly: ſo would Poetrye if there were the
like welcome and entertainment gyuen her by our
Engliſh Poets, without queſtion aſpyre to wonderfull
perfeſtion, and appeare farre more gorgeous and deleſt-
able among vs. Thus much I am bolde to ſay in
behalfe of Poetrie, not that I meane to call in queſtion
the reuerend and learned workes of Poetrie, written in
our tongue by men of rare iudgement, and moſt excellent Poets: but euen as it were by way of ſupplication
to the famous and learned Lawreat Maſters of Englande, that they would but conſult one halfe howre
with their heauenly Muſe, what credite they might
winne to theyr natiue ſpeeche, what enormities they
might wipe out of Engliſh Poetry, what a fitte vaine
they might frequent, wherein to ſhewe forth their worthie
faculties: if Engliſh Poetrie were truely reformed, and
ſome perfeſt platforme or *Proſodia* of verſifying were
by them ratifyed and ſette downe: eyther in immitation
of Greekes and Latines, or where it would ſkant abyde
the touch of theyr Rules, the like obſeruations ſeleſted
and eſtabliſhed by the naturall affeſtation of the
ſpeeche. Thus much I ſay, not to perſwade you that

are the fauourers of Englifhe Poetry but to mooue it
to you: beeing not the firfte that haue thought vpon
this matter, but one that by confent of others, haue
taken vppon me to lay it once again in your wayes, if
perhaps you may ftumble vppon it, and chance to looke
fo lowe from your diuine cogitations, when your Mufe
mounteth to the ftarres, and ranfacketh the Spheres of
heauen: whereby perhaps you may take compaffion of
noble Poetry, pittifullie mangled and defaced, by rude
fmatterers and barbarous immitatours of your worthy
ftudies. If the motion bee worthy your regard it is
enough to mooue it, if not, my wordes woulde fimply
preuaile in perfwading you, and therefore I reft vppon
thys onely requeft, that of your courtefies, you wyll
graunt paffage, vnder your fauourable corrections, for
this my fimple cenfure of Englifh Poetry, wherein if
you pleafe to runne it ouer, you fhall knowe breefely
myne opinion of the moft part of your accuftomed
Poets and particularly, in his place, the lyttle
fomewhat which I haue fifted out of my
weake brayne concerning thys
reformed verfifying.

VV: VV:

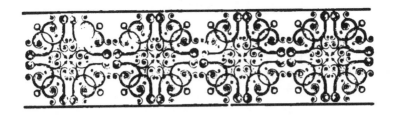

A Discourse of Eng=
lishe Poetrie.

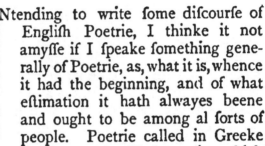

Ntending to write some discourse of Englishe Poetrie, I thinke it not amysse if I speake something generally of Poetrie, as, what it is, whence it had the beginning, and of what estimation it hath alwayes beene and ought to be among al sorts of people. Poetrie called in Greeke ποετρια, beeing deriued from the Verbe ποίεω, which signifieth in Latine *facere*, in Englishe, to make, may properly be defined, the arte of making: which word as it hath alwaies beene especially vsed of the best of our Englishe Poets, to expresse ye very faculty of speaking or wryting Poetically, so doth it in deede containe most fitly the whole grace and property of the same, ye more fullye and effectually then any other Englishe Verbe. That Poetry is an Arte, (or rather a more excellent thing then can be contayned wythin the compasse of Arte) though I neede not stande long to prooue, both the witnes of *Horace*, who wrote *de arte Poetica*, and of *Terence*, who calleth it *Artem Musicam*, and the very naturall property thereof may sufficiently declare: The beginning of it as appeareth by *Plato*, was of a vertuous and most deuout purpose,

who witneffeth, that by occafion of meeting of a great
company of young men, to folemnize ye feafts which
were called *Panegeryca*, and were wont to be celebrated euery fift yeere, there, they that were moft pregnant in wytt, and indued with great gyfts of wyfedome
and knowledge in Muficke aboue the reft did vfe
commonly to make goodly verfes, meafured according
to the fweeteft notes of Muficke, containing the prayfe
of fome noble vertue, or of immortalitie, or of fome
fuch thing of greateft eftimation: which vnto them
feemed, fo heauenly and ioyous a thing, that, thinking fuch men to be infpyrde with fome diuine inftinct
from heauen, they called them *Vates*.   So when other
among them of the fineft wits and apteft capacities
beganne in imitation of thefe to frame ditties of lighter
matters, and tuning them to the ftroake of fome of the
pleafanteft kind of Muficke, then began there to grow
a diftinction and great diuerfity betweene makers and
makers. Whereby (I take it) beganne thys difference:
that they which handled in the audience of the people,
graue and neceffary matters, were called wife men or
eloquent men, which they meant by *Vates*: and the
reft which fange of loue matters, or other lighter
deuifes alluring vnto pleafure and delight, were called
Poetæ or makers.   Thus it appeareth, both Eloquence
and Poetrie to haue had their beginning and originall
from thefe exercifes, beeing framed in fuch fweete
meafure of fentences and pleafant harmonie called
Pιθμος, which is an apt compofition of wordes or
claufes, drawing as it were by force ye hearers eares
euen whether foeuer it lyfteth: that *Plato* affirmeth
therein to be contained λοητεία an inchauntment, as
it were to perfwade them anie thing whether they would
or no.   And heerehence is fayde, that men were firft
withdrawne from a wylde and fauadge kinde of life, to
ciuillity and gentlenes, and ye right knowledge of
humanity by the force of this meafurable or tunable
fpeaking.
　　This opinion fhall you finde confirmed throughout

the whole workes of *Plato* and *Ariftotle*. And that fuch
was the eftimation of this Poetry at thofe times, that they
fuppofed all wifedome and knowledge to be included
myftically in that diuine inftinction, wherewith they
thought their *Uates* to bee infpyred. Wherevpon,
throughout the noble workes of thofe moft excellent
Philofophers before named, are the authorities of Poets
very often alledged. And *Cicero* in his *Tufculane* quef-
tions is of that minde, that a Poet cannot expreffe
verfes aboundantly, fufficiently, and fully, neither his
eloquence can flowe pleafauntly, or his wordes founde
well and plenteoufly, without celeftiall inftinction:
which Poets themfelues doo very often and gladlie
witnes of themfelues, as namely *Ouid* in. 6. *Fafto*:
Est deus in nobis Agitante callefcimus illo. etc. Wherevnto I doubt not equally to adioyne the authoritye of
our late famous Englifh Poet, who wrote the *Sheepheards Calender*, where lamenting the decay of Poetry,
at thefe dayes, faith moft fweetely to the fame.

Then make thee winges of thine afpyring wytt,

And whence thou cameft flye back to heauen apace. etc.

   Whofe fine poeticall witt, and moft exquifite learning,
as he fhewed aboundantly in that peece of worke, in my
iudgment inferiour to the workes neither of *Theocritus*
in Greeke, nor *Virgill* in Latine, whom hee narrowly
immitateth: fo I nothing doubt, but if his other workes
were common abroade, which are as I thinke in ye clofe
cuftodie of certaine his freends, we fhould haue of our
owne Poets, whom wee might matche in all refpects
with the beft. And among all other his workes whatfoeuer, I would wyfh to haue the fight of hys *Englifh
Poet*, which his freend *E. K.* did once promife to
publifhe, which whether he performed or not, I knowe
not, if he did, my happe hath not beene fo good as
yet to fee it.
   But to returne to the eftimation of Poetry. Befides
ye great and profitable fruites contained in Poetry, for

the inftruction of manners and precepts of good life
(for that was cheefly refpected in the firft age of Poetry)
this is alfo added to the eternall commendations of
that noble faculty: that Kinges and Princes, great and
famous men, did euer encourage, mayntaine, and reward
Poets in al ages: becaufe they were thought onely to
haue the whole power in their handes, of making men
either immortally famous for their valiaunt exploytes
and vertuous exercifes, or perpetually infamous for
their vicious liues. Wherevppon it is faid of *Achilles*,
that this onely vantage he had of *Hector*, that it was
his fortune to be extolled and renowned by the heauenly verfe of *Homer*. And as *Tully* recordeth to be
written of *Alexander*, that with natural teares he wept
ouer *Achilles* Tombe, in ioy that he conceiued at the
confideration, howe it was his happe to be honoured
wyth fo diuine a worke, as *Homers* was. *Ariftotle*, a
moft prudent and learned Philofopher, beeing appointed
Schoolemafter to the young Prince *Alexander*, thought
no worke fo meete to be reade vnto a King, as the
worke of *Homer*: wherein the young Prince being by
him inftructed throughly, found fuch wonderfull delight
in the fame when hee came to maturity, that hee would
not onely haue it with him in all his iourneyes, but in
his bedde alfo vnder his pyllowe, to delight him and
teach him both nights and dayes. The fame is
reported of noble *Scipio*, who finding the two Bookes
of *Homer* in the fpoyle of Kyng *Darius*, efteemed them
as wonderfull precious Iewelles, making one of them
his companion for the night, the other for the day.
And not onely was he thus affected to yat one peece
or parte of Poetry, but fo generally he loued the profef-
fors thereof, that in his moft ferious affayres, and hot-
teft warres againft *Numantia* and *Carthage* he could
no whitte be without that olde Poet *Ennius* in his
company. But to fpeake of all thofe noble and wyfe
Princes, who bare fpeciall fauour and countenaunce to
Poets, were tedious, and would require a rehearfall of
all fuch, in whofe time there grewe any to credite and

eftimation in that faculty. Thus farre therefore may
fuffice for the eftimation of Poets. Nowe I thinke
moft meete, to fpeake fomewhat, concerning what hath
beene the vfe of Poetry, and wherin it rightly confifted,
and whereof confequently it obteyned fuch eftimation.
To begin therefore with the firft that was firft worthe-
lye memorable in the excellent gyft of Poetrye, the
beft wryters agree that it was *Orpheus*, who by ,the
fweete gyft of his heauenly Poetry, withdrew men from
raungyng vncertainly, and wandring brutifhly about,
and made them gather together, and keepe company,
made houfes, and kept fellowfhippe together, who
therefore is reported (as *Horace* fayth) to affwage the
fiercenefle of Tygers, and mooue the harde Flynts.
After him was *Amphion*, who was the firft that caufed
Citties to bee builded, and men therein to liue decently
and orderly according to lawe and right. Next, was
Tyrtæus, who began to practife warlike defences, to
keepe back enemies, and faue themfelues from inuafion
of foes. In thys place I thinke were moft conuenient
to rehearfe that auncient Poet *Pyndarus*: but of the
certaine time wherein he flourifhed, I am not very
certaine: but of the place where he continued mofte,
it fhoulde feeme to be the Citty of *Thebes*, by *Plinie*
who reporteth, that *Alexander* in facking the fame
Cittie, woulde not fuffer the houfe wherein he dwelt to
be fpoyled as all the reft were. After thefe was *Homer*,
who as it were in one fumme comprehended all knowledge, wifedome, learning, and pollicie, that was incident to the capacity of man. And who fo lifte to take
viewe of hys two Bookes, one of his *Iliades*, the other
his *Odifsea*, fhall throughly perceiue what the right vfe
of Poetry is: which indeede is to mingle profite with
pleafure, and fo to delight the Reader with pleafantnes
of hys Arte, as in ye meane time, his mind may be well
inftructed with knowledge and wifedome. For fo did
that worthy Poet frame thofe his two workes, that in
reading the firft, that is his *Iliads*, by declaring and
fetting forth fo liuely the Grecians affembly againft

Troy, together with their proweffe and fortitude againſt their foes, a Prince fhall learne not onely courage, and valiantneffe, but difcretion alfo and pollicie to encounter with his enemies, yea a perfect forme of wyfe confulta-tions, with his Captaines, and exhortations to the people, with other infinite commodities.

Agayne, in the other part, wherein are defcribed the manifold and daungerous aduentures of *Vliſſes*, may a man learne many noble vertues: and alfo learne to efcape and auoyde the fubtyll practifes, and perrilous entrappinges of naughty perfons: and not onely this, but in what fort alfo he may deale to knowe and per-ceiue the affections of thofe which be neere vnto him, and moſt familiar with him, the better to put them in truſt with his matters of waight and importaunce. Therefore I may boldly fette downe thys to be the trueſt, auncienteſt and beſt kinde of Poetry, to direct ones endeuour alwayes to that marke, that with delight they may euermore adioyne commoditie to theyr Readers: which becaufe I grounde vpon *Homer* the Prince of all Poets, therefore haue I alledged the order of his worke, as an authority fufficiently proouing this aſſertion.

Nowe what other Poets which followed him, and beene of greateſt fame, haue doone for the moſte parte in their feuerall workes I wyll briefely, and as my flender ability wyll ferue me declare. But by my leaue, I muſt content my felfe to fpeake not of all, but of fuch as my felfe haue feene, and beene beſt acquainted withall, and thofe not all nor the moſte part of the auncient Grecians, of whom I know not how many there were, but thefe of the Latiniſts, which are of greateſt fame and moſt obuious among vs.

Thus much I can fay, that *Ariſtotle* reporteth none to haue greatly flourifhed in Greece, at leaſt wyfe not left behynd them any notable memoriall, before the time of *Homer*. And *Tully* fayth as much, that there were none wrytt woorth the reading twyce in the Romaine tongue, before ye Poet *Ennius*. And furely

as the very fumme or cheefeft effence of Poetry, dyd
alwayes for the moft part confift in delighting the
readers or hearers wyth pleafure, fo as the number of
Poets increafed, they ftyll inclyned thys way rather
then the other, fo that moft of them had fpeciall
regarde, to the pleafantneffe of theyr fine conceytes,
whereby they might drawe mens mindes into admiration of theyr inuentions, more then they had to the
profitte or commoditye that the Readers fhoulde
reape by their works. And thus as I fuppofe came
it to paffe among them, that for the moft part of them,
they would not write one worke contayning fome ferious
matter: but for the fame they wold likewife powre foorth
as much of fome wanton or laciuious inuention. Yet
fome of the auncienteft fort of Grecians, as it feemeth
were not fo much difpofed to vayne delectation: as
Ariftotle fayth of *Empedocles*, that in hys iudgment he
was onely a naturall Philofopher, no Poet at all, nor
that he was like vnto *Homer* in any thing but hys
meeter, or number of feete, that is, that hee wrote in
verfe. After the time of *Homer*, there began the firfte
Comedy wryters, who compyled theyr workes in a better
ftile which continued not long, before it was expelled
by penalty, for fcoffing too broade at mens manners,
and the priuie reuengements which the Poets vfed
againft their ill wyllers. Among thefe was *Eupolis*,
Cratinus, and *Ariftophenes*, but afterward the order of
thys wryting Comedies was reformed and made more
plaufible: then wrytte *Plato*, *Comicus*, *Menander*, and
I knowe not who more.
  There be many moft profitable workes, of like antiquity, or rather before them, of the Tragedy writers:
as of *Euripides*, and *Sophocles*, then was there *Phoci-
tides* and *Theagines*, with many other: which Tragedies
had their inuention by one *Thefpis*, and were pollifhed
and amended by *Æfchilus*. The profitte or difcom-
moditie which aryfeth by the vfe of thefe Comedies and
Tragedies, which is moft, hath beene long in contro-
uerfie, and is fore vrged among vs at thefe dayes: what

I thinke of the fame, perhaps I fhall breefely declare anon.

Nowe concerning the Poets which wrote in homely manner, as they pretended, but indeede, with great pythe and learned iudgment, fuch as were the wryters of Sheepeheards talke and of hufbandly precepts, who were among the Grecians that excelled, befides *Theocritus* and *Hefiodus* I know not, of whom the firft, what profitable workes he left to pofterity, befides hys *Idillia* or contentions of Goteheards, tending moft to delight, and pretty inuentions, I can not tell. The other, no doubt for his Argument he tooke in hande, dealt very learnedly and profitably, that is, in precepts of Hufbandry, but yet fo as he myxed much wanton ftuffe among the reft.

The firft wryters of Poetry among the Latines, fhoulde feeme to be thofe, which excelled in the framing of Commedies, and that they continued a long time without any notable memory of other Poets. Among whom, the cheefeft that we may fee or heare tell of, were thefe. *Ennius, Cæcilius, Næuius, Licinius, Attilius, Turpitius, Trabea, Lufcius, Plautus*, and *Terens*. Of whom thefe two laft named, haue beene euer fince theyr time moft famous, and to thefe dayes are efteemed, as greate helpes and furtheraunces to the obtayning of good Letters. But heere cannot I ftaye to fpeake of the moft famous, renowned and excellent, that euer writte among the Latine Poets, *P. Virgill*, who performed the very fame in that tongue, which *Homer* had doone in Greeke: or rather better if better might as *Sex. Propert.* in his *Elegies* gallantly recordeth in his praife, *Nefcio quid magis nafcitur Iliade*. Vnder the perfon of *Æneas* he expreffeth the valoure of a worthy Captaine and valiaunt Gouernour, together with the perrilous aduentures of warre, and polliticke deuifes at all affayes. And as he immitateth *Homer* in that worke, fo dooth he likewyfe followe the very fteps of *Theocritus*, in his moft pythy inuentions of his *Æglogues*: and likewyfe *Hefiodus* in h.s *Georgicks* or bookes of

Hufbandry, but yet more grauely, and in a more decent
ftyle. But notwithftanding hys fage grauity and wonderfull wifedome, dyd he not altogether reftrayne his
vayne, but that he would haue a caft at fome wanton
and fkant comely an Argument, if indeede fuch trifles
as be fathered vppon him were his owne. There followed after him, very many rare and excellent Poets,
whereof the moft part writt light matters, as *Epigrammes* and *Elegies*, with much pleafant dalliance, among
whom may be accounted *Propertius, Tibullus, Catullus*,
with diuers whom *Ouid* fpeaketh of in diuers places of
his workes. Then are there two Hyftoricall Poets, no
leffe profitable then delightfome to bee read: *Silius* and
Lucanus: the one declaring the valiant proweffe of two
noble Captaines, one enemie to the other, that is, *Scipio*
and *Haniball*: the other likewife, the fortitude of two
expert warriours (yet more lamentably then the other
becaufe thefe warres were ciuill) *Pompey* and *Cæfar.*
The next in tyme (but as moft men doo account, and
fo did he himfelfe) the fecond in dignity, we will adioyne *Ouid*, a moft learned, and exquifite Poet. The
worke of greateft profitte which he wrote, was his
Booke of *Metamorphofis*, which though it confifted of
fayned Fables for the moft part, and poeticall inuentions,
yet beeing moralized according to his meaning, and the
trueth of euery tale beeing difcouered, it is a worke of
exceeding wyfedome and founde iudgment. If one
lyft in like manner, to haue knowledge and perfect
intelligence of thofe rytes and ceremonies which were
obferued after the Religion of the Heathen, no more
profitable worke for that purpofe, then his bookes
De faftis. The reft of his dooinges, though they tende
to the vayne delights of loue and dalliaunce (except
his *Triftibus* wherein he bewayleth hys exile) yet furely
are mixed with much good counfayle and profitable
leffons if they be wifely and narrowly read. After his
time I know no worke of any great fame, till the time
of *Horace*, a Poet not of the fmootheft ftyle, but in
fharpneffe of wytt inferiour to none, and one to whom

all the reft both before his time and fince, are very much
beholding. About the fame time *Iuuenall* and *Perfius*,
then *Martial*, *Seneca* a moft excellent wryter of Tragedies, *Boetius*, *Lucretius*, *Statius*, *Val*: *Flaccus*, *Manilius*,
Aufonius, *Claudian*, and many other, whofe iuft times
and feuerall woorkes to fpeake of in this place, were
neither much needefull, nor altogeather tollerable,
becaufe I purpofed an other argument. Onely I will
adde two of later times, yet not farre inferiour to the
moft of them aforefayde, *Pallengenius*, and *Bap. Man-
tuanus*, and for a finguler gyft in a fweete Heroicall
verfe, match with them *Chr. Oclan.* the Authour of
our *Anglorum Prœlia.* But nowe leaft I ftray too farre
from my purpofe, I wyl come to our Englifh Poets, to
whom I would I were able to yeelde theyr deferued
commendations: and affoorde them that cenfure, which
I know many woulde, which can better, if they were
nowe to write in my fteede.

I know no memorable worke written by any Poet in
our Englifh fpeeche, vntill twenty yeeres paft: where
although Learning was not generally decayde at any time,
efpecially fince the Conqueft of King *William* Duke of
Normandy, as it may appeare by many famous works
and learned bookes (though not of this kinde) wrytten
by Byfhoppes and others: yet furelye that Poetry was
in fmall price among them, it is very manifeft, and no
great maruayle, for euen that light of Greeke and Latine
Poets which they had, they much contemned, as appeareth by theyr rude verfifying, which of long time
was vfed (a barbarous vfe it was) wherin they conuerted
the naturall property of the fweete Latine verfe, to be
a balde kinde of ryming, thinking nothing to be learnedly written in verfe, which fell not out in ryme, that
is, in wordes whereof the middle worde of eche verfe
fhould found a like with the laft, or of two verfes, the
ende of both fhould fall in the like letters as thus.

O malè viuentes, verfus audite fequentes.

And thus likewyfe.

Propter hæc et alia dogmata doctorum
Reor effe melius et magis decorum:
Quifque fuam habeat, et non proximorum.

This brutifh Poetrie, though it had not the beginning in this Countrey, yet fo hath it beéne affected heere, that the infection thereof would neuer (nor I thinke euer will) be rooted vppe againe: I meane this tynkerly verfe which we call ryme: Mafter *Afcham* fayth, that it firft began to be followed and maintained among the *Hunnes* and *Gothians*, and other barbarous Nations, who with the decay of all good learning, brought it into *Italy*: from thence it came into *Fraunce*, and fo to *Germany*, at laft conueyed into *England*, by men indeede of great wifedome and learning, but not confiderate nor circumfpect in that behalfe. But of this I muft intreate more heereafter.

Henry the firft King of that name in England, is wonderfully extolled, in all auncient Recordes of memory, for hys finguler good learning, in all kinde of noble ftudies, in fo much as he was named by his furname *Beaucleark*, as much to fay, as *Fayreclerke* (whereof perhappes came ye name of *Fayreclowe*) what knowledge hee attained in the fkyll of Poetry, I am not able to fay, I report his name for proofe, that learning in this Country was not little efteemed of at that rude time, and that like it is, among other ftudies, a King would not neglect the faculty of Poetry. The firft of our Englifh Poets that I haue heard of, was *Iohn Gower*, about the time of king *Rychard* the feconde, as it fhould feeme by certayne coniectures bothe a Knight, and queftionleffe a finguler well learned man: whofe workes I could wyfh they were all whole and perfect among vs, for no doubt they contained very much deepe knowledge and delight: which may be gathered by his freend *Chawcer*, who fpeaketh of him oftentimes, in

diuer[s] places of hys workes. *Chawcer*, who for that
excellent fame which hee obtayned in his Poetry, was
alwayes accounted the God of Englifh Poets (fuch a
tytle for honours fake hath beene giuen him) was next
after, if not equall in time to *Gower*, and hath left many
workes, both for delight and profitable knowledge, farre
exceeding any other that as yet euer fince hys time
directed theyr ftudies that way. Though the manner
of hys ftile may feeme blunte and courfe to many fine
Englifh eares at thefe dayes, yet in trueth, if it be equally
pondered, and with good iudgment aduifed, and confirmed with the time wherein he wrote, a man fhall
perceiue thereby euen a true picture or perfect fhape
of a right Poet. He by his delightfome vayne, fo
gulled the eares of men with his deuifes, that, although
corruption bare fuch fway in moft matters, that learning
and truth might fkant bee admitted to fhewe it felfe,
yet without controllment, myght hee gyrde at the vices
and abufes of all ftates, and gawle with very fharpe and
eger inuentions, which he did fo learnedly and plea-
fantly, that none therefore would call him into queftion.
For fuch was his bolde fpyrit, that what enormities he
faw in any, he would not fpare to pay them home,
eyther in playne words, or els in fome prety and pleafant
couert, that the fimpleft might efpy him.

Neere in time vnto him was *Lydgate* a Poet, furely
for good proportion of his verfe, and meetely currant
ftyle, as the time affoorded comparable with *Chawcer*,
yet more occupyed in fuperfticious and odde matters,
then was requefite in fo good a wytte: which, though
he handled them commendably, yet the matters themfelues beeing not fo commendable, hys eftimation hath
beene the leffe. The next of our auncient Poets, that
I can tell of, I fuppofe to be *Pierce Ploughman*, who
in hys dooinges is fomewhat harfhe and obfcure, but
indeede a very pithy wryter, and (to hys commendation
I fpeake it) was the firft that I haue feene, that obferued
ye quantity of our verfe without the curiofity of Ryme.

Since thefe I knowe none other tyll the time of

Skelton, who writ in the time of Kyng *Henry* the eyght, who as indeede he obtayned the Lawrell Garland, fo may I wyth good ryght yeelde him the title of a Poet: hee was doubtles a pleafant conceyted fellowe, and of a very fharpe wytte, exceeding bolde, and would nyppe to the very quicke where he once fette holde. Next hym I thynke I may place mafter *George Gafkoyne*, as painefull a Souldier in the affayres of hys Prince and Country, as he was a wytty Poet in his wryting: whofe commendations, becaufe I found in one of better iudgment then my felfe, I wyl fette downe hys wordes, and fuppreffe myne owne, of hym thus wryteth *E. K.* vppon the ninth *Æglogue* of the new Poet.

Mafter *George Gafkoyne* a wytty Gentleman and the very cheefe of our late rymers, who and if fome partes of learning wanted not (albeit is well knowne he altogether wanted not learning) no doubt would haue attayned to the excellencye of thofe famous Poets. For gyfts of wytt, and naturall promptnes appeare in him aboundantly. I might next fpeake of the dyuers workes of the olde Earle of *Surrey*: of the L. *Vaus*, of *Norton*, of *Briftow*, *Edwardes*, *Tuffer*, *Churchyard*. *VVyl*: *Hunnis*: *Haiwood*: *Sand*: *Hyll*: *S. Y. M. D.* and many others, but to fpeake of their feuerall gyfts, and aboundant fkyll fhewed forth by them in many pretty and learned workes, would make my difcourfe much more tedious.

I may not omitte the deferued commendations of many honourable and noble Lordes, and Gentlemen, in her Maiefties Courte, which in the rare deuifes of Poetry, haue beene and yet are moft excellent fkylfull, among whom, the right honourable Earle of *Oxford* may challenge to him felfe the tytle of ye moft excellent among the reft. I can no longer forget thofe learned Gentlemen which tooke fuch profitable paynes in translating the Latine Poets into our Englifh tongue, whofe defertes in that behalfe are more then I can vtter. Among thefe, I euer efteemed, and while I lyue, in my conceyt I fhall account Mafter *D. Phaer*: without doubt

the beft: who as indeede hee had the beft peece of
Poetry whereon to fette a moft gallant verfe, fo performed he it accordingly, and in fuch fort, as in my
confcience I thinke would fcarcely be doone againe, if
it were to doo again. Notwithftanding, I fpeak it but
as myne own fancy, not preiudiciall to thofe that lift to
thinke otherwyfe. Hys worke whereof I fpeake, is the
englifhing of *Æneidos* of *Virgill*, fo farre foorth as it
pleafed God to fpare him life, which was to the halfe
parte of the tenth Booke, the reft beeing fince wyth no
leffe commendations finifhed, by that worthy fcholler
and famous Phifition Mafter *Thomas Twyne.*

Equally with him may I well adioyne Mafter *Arthur
Golding*, for hys labour in englifhing *Ouids Metamorphofis*, for which Gentleman, furely our Country hath
for many refpects greatly to gyue God thankes: as for
him which hath taken infinite paynes without ceafing,
trauelleth as yet indefatigably, and is addicted without
fociety, by his continuall laboure, to profit this nation
and fpeeche in all kind of good learning. The next,
very well deferueth Mafter *Barnabe Googe* to be placed,
as a painefull furtherer of learning: hys helpe to Poetry
befides hys owne deuifes, as the tranflating of *Pallengenius. Lodiac. Abraham Flemming* as in many prety
Poefis of hys owne, fo in tranflating hath doone to hys
commendations. To whom I would heere adioyne one
of hys name, whom I know to haue excelled, as well
in all kinde of learning as in Poetry moft efpecially,
and would appeare fo, if the dainty morfelles, and fine
poeticall inuentions of hys, were as common abroade
as I knowe they be among fome of hys freendes. I wyl
craue leaue of the laudable Authors of *Seneca* in Englifh, of the other partes of *Ouid*, of *Horace*, of *Mantuan*,
and diuers other, becaufe I would haften to ende thys
rehearfall, perhappes offenfyue to fome, whom eyther
by forgetfulnes, or want of knowledge, I muft needes
ouer paffe.

And once againe, I am humbly to defire pardon of
the learned company of Gentlemen Schollers, and

ftudents of the Vniuerfities, and Innes of Courte, yf I
omitte theyr feuerall commendations in this place,
which I knowe a great number of them haue worthely
deferued, in many rare deuifes, and finguler inuentions
of Poetrie: for neither hath it beene my good happe,
to hauc feene all which I haue hearde of, neyther is
my abyding in fuch place, where I can with facility get
knowledge of their workes.

One Gentleman notwithftanding among them may I
not ouerflyppe, fo farre reacheth his fame, and fo worthy
is he, if hee haue not already, to weare the Lawrell
wreathe, Mafter *George VVhetftone*, a man fingularly
well fkyld in this faculty of Poetrie: To him I wyl
ioyne *Anthony Munday*, an earneft traueller in this
arte, and in whofe name I haue feene very excellent
workes, among which furely, the moft exquifite vaine
of a witty poeticall heade is fhewed in the fweete fobs
of Sheepheardes and Nymphes: a worke well worthy
to be viewed, and to bee efteemed as very rare Poetrie.
With thefe I may place *Iohn Graunge, Knyght, VVyl-
mott, Darrell, F. C. F. K. G. B.* and many other,
whofe names come not nowe to my remembraunce.

This place haue I purpofely referued for one, who
if not only, yet in my iudgement principally deferueth
the tytle of the righteft Englifh Poet, that euer I read:
that is, the Author of the Sheepeheardes Kalender,
intituled to the woorthy Gentleman Mafter *Phillip
Sydney*, whether it was Mafter *Sp.* or what rare Scholler in Pembrooke Hall foeuer, becaufe himfelf and his
freendes, for what refpect I knowe not, would not
reueale it, I force not greatly to fette downe: forry I
am that I can not find none other with whom I might
couple him in this *Catalogue*, in his rare gyft of Poetry:
although one there is, though nowe long fince, ferioufly
occupied in grauer ftudies, (Mafter *Gabriell Haruey*)
yet, as he was once his moft fpecial freende and fellow
Poet, fo becaufe he hath taken fuch paynes, not onely
in his Latin Poetry (for which he enioyed great commendations of the beft both in iudgment and dignity in

thys Realme) but alfo to reforme our Englifh verfe, and
to beautify the fame with braue deuifes, of which I
thinke the cheefe lye hidde in hatefull obfcurity: therefore wyll I aduenture to fette them together, as two of
the rareft witts, and learnedft mafters of Poetrie in
England. Whofe worthy and notable fkyl in this
faculty, I would wyfh if their high dignities and ferious
bufineffes would permit, they would ftyll graunt to bee
a furtheraunce to that reformed kinde of Poetry, which
Mafter *Haruey* did once beginne to ratify: and furely
in mine opinion, if hee had chofen fome grauer matter,
and handled but with halfe that fkyll, which I knowe
he could haue doone, and not powred it foorth at a
venture, as a thinge betweene·ieft and earneft, it had
taken greater effect then it did.

As for the other Gentleman, if it would pleafe him
or hys freendes to let thofe excellent *Poemes*, whereof
I know he hath plenty, come abroad, as his Dreames,
his Legends, his Court of *Cupid*, his English Poet with
other: he fhoulde not onely ftay the rude pens of my
felfe and others, but alfo fatiffye the thirfty defires of
many which defire nothing more, then to fee more of
hys rare inuentions. If I ioyne to Mafter *Haruey* hys
two Brethren, I am affured, though they be both bufied
with great and waighty callinges (the one a godly and
learned Diuine, the other a famous and fkylfull Phifition)
yet if they lyfted to fette to their helping handes to
Poetry, they would as much beautify and adorne it as
any others.

If I let paffe the vncountable rabble of ryming Ballet
makers and compylers of fenceleffe fonets, who be moft
bufy, to ftuffe euery ftall full of groffe deuifes and vn-
learned Pamphlets: I truft I fhall with the beft fort be
held excufed. Nor though many fuch can frame an
Alehoufe fong of fiue of fixe fcore verfes, hobbling vppon
fome tune of a Northen Iygge, or Robyn hoode, or
La lubber etc. And perhappes obferue iuft number of
fillables, eyght in one line, fixe in an other, and there
withall an A to make a iercke in the ende: yet if thefe

might be accounted Poets (as it is fayde fome of them make meanes to be promoted to ye Lawrell) furely we fhall fhortly haue whole fwarmes of Poets: and euery one that can frame a Booke in Ryme, though for want of matter, it be but in commendations of Copper nofes or Bottle Ale, wyll catch at the Garlande due to Poets: whofe potticall poeticall (I fhould fay) heades, I would wyfhe, at their worfhipfull comencements might in fteede of Lawrell, be gorgioufly garnifhed with fayre greene Barley, in token of their good affection to our Englifhe Malt. One fpeaketh thus homely of them, with whofe words I wyll content my felfe for thys time, be-caufe I woulde not bee too broade wyth them in myne owne fpeeche.

In regarde (he meaneth of the learned framing the newe Poets workes which writt the Sheepheardes Calender.) I fcorne and fpue out the rakehelly rout of our ragged Rymers, (for fo themfelues vfe to hunt the Letter) which without learning boafte, without iudgment iangle, without reafon rage and fume, as if fome inftinct of poeticall fpyrite had newlie rauifhed them, aboue the meaneffe of common capacity. And beeing in the midft of all their brauery, fuddainly for want of matter or of Ryme, or hauing forgotten their former conceyt, they feeme to be fo payned and trauelled in theyr remembraunce, as it were a woman in Chyldbyrth, or as that fame *Pythia* when the traunce came vpon her. *Os rabidum fera corda domans etc.*

Hus farre foorth haue I aduentured to fette downe parte of my fimple iudgement concerning thofe Poets, with whom for the moft part I haue beene acquainted through myne owne reading: which though it may feeme fomething impertinent to the tytle of my Booke, yet I truft the courteous Readers wyll pardon me, confidering that poetry is not of that grounde and antiquity in our Englifh tongue, but that fpeaking thereof only as it is Englifh, would feeme like vnto the drawing of ones pycture without a heade.

Nowe therefore by your gentle patience, wyll I wyth like breuity make tryall, what I can fay concerning our Englifhe Poetry, firft in the matter thereof, then in the forme, that is, the manner of our verfe: yet fo as I muft euermore haue recourfe to thofe times and wryters, whereon the Englifh poetry taketh as it were the difcent and proprietye.

Englifh Poetry therefore beeing confidered according to common cuftome and auncient vfe, is, where any worke is learnedly compiled in meafurable fpeeche, and framed in wordes contayning number or proportion of iuft fyllables, delighting the readers or hearers as well by the apt and decent framing of wordes in equall refemblance of quantity, commonly called verfe, as by the fkyllfull handling of the matter whereof it is intreated. I fpake fomewhat of the beginning of thys meafuring of wordes in iuft number, taken out of *Plato*: and indeede the regarde of true quantity in Letters and fyllables, feemeth not to haue been much vrged before the time of *Homer* in Greece, as *Ariftotle* witneffeth.

The matters whereof verfes were firft made, were eyther exhortations to vertue, dehortations from vice, or the prayfes of fome laudable thing. From thence they beganne to vfe them in exercifes of immitating fome vertuous and wife man at their feaftes: where as fome one fhoulde be appointed to reprefent an other mans perfon of high eftimation, and he fang fine ditties and wittie fentences, tunably to their Mufick notes. Of thys fprang the firft kinde of Comedyes, when they beganne to bring into thefe exercifes, more perfons then one, whofe fpeeches were deuifed Dyalogue wife, in aunfwering one another. And of fuch like exer-

cifes, or as fome wyll needes haue it, long before the
other, began the firft Tragedies, and were fo called of
τραγος, becaufe the Actor when he began to play his
part, flewe and offered a Goate to their Goddeffe: but
Commedies tooke their name of κομάζειν και ἀδειν
comefsatum ire, to goe a feafting, becaufe they vfed to
goe in proceffion with their fport about the Citties and
Villages, mingling much pleafaunt myrth wyth theyr
graue Religion, and feafting cheerefully together wyth
as great ioy as might be deuifed. But not long after
(as one delight draweth another) they began to inuent
new perfons and newe matters for their Comedies,
fuch as the deuifers thought meeteft to pleafe the
peoples vaine: And from thefe, they beganne to prefent in fhapes of men, the natures of vertues and
vices, and affections and quallities incident to men,
as Iuftice, Temperance, Pouerty, Wrathe, Vengeaunce,
Sloth, Valiantnes, and fuch like, as may appeare by
the auncient workes of *Ariftophanes.* There grewe at
laft to be a greater diuerfitye betweene Tragedy wryters
and Comedy wryters, the one expreffing onely forrow-
full and lamentable Hyftories, bringing in the perfons
of Gods and Goddeffes, Kynges and Queenes, and
great ftates, whofe parts were cheefely to expreffe moft
miferable calamities and dreadfull chaunces, which
increafed worfe and worfe, tyll they came to the moft
wofull plight that might be deuifed.

The Comedies on the other fide, were directed to a
contrary ende, which beginning doubtfully, drewe to
fome trouble or turmoyle, and by fome lucky chaunce
alwayes ended to the ioy and appeafement of all
parties. Thys diftinction grewe as fome holde opinion,
by immitation of the workes of *Homer*: for out of his
Iliads, the Tragedy wryters founde dreadfull euents,
whereon to frame their matters, and the other out of
hys *Odyffea* tooke arguments of delight, and pleafant
ending after dangerous and troublefome doubtes. So
that, though there be many fortes of poeticall wrytings,
and Poetry is not debarred from any matter, which

may be exprelfed by penne or fpeeche, yet for the
better vnderftanding, and breefer method of thys
difcourfe, I may comprehende the fame in three fortes,
which are Comicall, Tragicall, Hiftori[c]all. Vnder the
firft, may be contained all fuch *Epigrammes*, *Elegies*
and delectable ditties, which Poets haue deuifed re-
fpecting onely the delight thereof: in the feconde, all
dolefull complaynts, lamentable chaunces, and what
foeuer is poetically exprelfed in forrow and heauines.
In the third, we may comprife, the refte of all fuch
matters, which is indifferent betweene the other two,
doo commonly occupy the pennes of Poets: fuch, are
the poeticall compyling of Chronicles, the freendly
greetings betweene freendes, and very many fortes
befides, which for the better diftinction may be referred to one of thefe three kindes of Poetry. But once
againe, leaft my difcourfe runne too farre awry, wyll
I buckle my felfe more neerer to Englifh Poetry: the
vfe wherof, becaufe it is nothing different from any
other, I thinke beft to confirme by the teftimony of
Horace, a man worthy to beare authority in this
matter: whofe very opinion is this, that the perfect
perfection of poetrie is this, to mingle delight with
profitt in fuch wyfe, that a Reader might by his reading be pertaker of bothe, which though I touched in
the beginning, yet I thought good to alledge in this
place for more confirmation thereof fome of hys owne
wordes. In his treatife *de arte Poetica*, thus hee fayth.

Aut prodeffe volunt aut delectare poetæ,

Aut fimul et iucunda et idonea dicere vitæ.

As much to faie: All Poets defire either by their
works to profitt or delight men, or els to ioyne both
profitable and pleafant leffons together for the inftruction of life.

And again

Omne tulit punƐtum qui mifcuit vtile dulci,
LeƐtorum deleƐtando pariterque mouendo.

That is, He miffeth nothing of his marke which
ioyneth profitt with delight, as well delighting his
Readers, as profiting them with counfell. And that
whole Epiftle which hee wryt of his Arte of Poetrie,
among all the parts thereof, runneth cheefelie vppon
this, that whether the argument which the Poet hand-
leth, be of thinges doone, or fained inuentions, yet
that they fhould beare fuch an Image of trueth, that
as they delight they may likewife profitt. For thefe
are his wordes. *FiƐta voluptatis caufa fint proxima*
veris. Let thinges that are faigned for pleafures fake,
haue a neere refemblance of ye truth. This precept
may you perceiue to bee moft duelie obferued of
Chawcer: for who could with more delight, prefcribe
fuch wholfome counfaile and fage aduife, where he
feemeth onelie to refpect the profitte of his leffons and
inftructions? or who coulde with greater wifedome, or
more pithie fkill, vnfold fuch pleafant and delightfome
matters of mirth, as though they refpected nothing,
but the telling of a merry tale? fo that this is the
very grounde of right poetrie, to giue profitable counfaile, yet fo as it muft be mingled with delight. For
among all the auncient works of poetrie, though the
moft of them incline much to that part of delighting
men with pleafant matters of fmall importaunce, yet
euen in the vaineft trifles among them, there is not
forgotten fome profitable counfaile, which a man may
learne, either by flatte precepts which therein are prefcribed, or by loathing fuch vile vices, the enormities
whereof they largelie difcouer. For furelie, I am of
this opinion, that the wantoneft Poets of all, in their
moft laciuious workes wherein they bufied themfelues,
fought rather by that meanes to withdraw mens
mindes (efpeciallie the beft natures) from fuch foule
vices, then to allure them to imbrace fuch beaftly
follies as they detected.

Horace fpeaking of the generall dueties of Poets,
fayth, *Os tenerum pueri balbumque poeta fugitat*, and
manie more wordes concerning the profitte to be hadde
out of Poets, which becaufe I haue fome of them com-
prifed into an Englifh tranflation of that learned and
famous knight, Sir *Thomas Elyot*, I wyll fet downe his
wordes.

> The Poet fafhioneth by fome pleafant meane,
> The fpeeche of children ftable and vnfure:
> Gulling their eares from wordes and thinges vncleane,
> Giuing to them precepts that are pure:
> Rebuking enuy and wrath if it dure:
> Thinges well donne he can by example commend,
> To needy and ficke he doth alfo his cure
> To recomfort if ought he can amende.

And manie other like wordes are in that place of *Horace* to like effect. Therefore poetrie, as it is of it felfe,
without abufe is not onely not vnprofitable to the liues
and ftudies of menne, but wonderfull commendable and
of great excellencie. For nothing can be more acceptable to men, or rather to be wifhed, then fweete allure-
ments to vertues, and commodious caueates from vices?
of which Poetrie is exceeding plentifull, powring into
gentle witts, not roughly and tirannicallie, but it is were
with a louing authoritie. Nowe if the ill and vndecent
prouocations, whereof fome vnbridled witts take occafion
by the reading of laciuious Poemes, bee obiected: fuch
as are *Ouids* loue Bookes, and *Elegies*, *Tibullus*, *Catullus*, and *Martials* workes, with the Comedies for the
moft part of *Plautus* and *Terence*: I thinke it eafily
aunfwered. For though it may not iuftlie be denied,
that thefe workes are indeede very Poetrie, yet that
Poetrie in them is not the effentiall or formall matter
or caufe of the hurt therein might be affirmed, and
although that reafon fhould come fhort, yet this might
be fufficient, that the workes themfelues doo not corrupt, but the abufe of the vfers, who vndamaging their

owne difpofitions, by reading the difcoueries of vices,
refemble foolifh folke, who comming into a Garden
without anie choife or circumfpection tread downe the
faireft flowers, and wilfullie thruft their fingers among
the nettles.

And furelie to fpeake what I verelie thinke, this is
mine opinion: that one hauing fufficient fkyll, to reade
and vnderftand thofe workes, and yet no ftaie of him
felfe to auoyde inconueniences, which the remembraunce
of vnlawfull things may ftirre vppe in his minde, he, in
my iudgement, is wholy to bee reputed a laciuious difpofed perfonne, whom the recitall of fins whether it be
in a good worke or a badde, or vppon what occafion
foeuer, wyll not ftaie him but prouoke him further vnto
them. Contrariwife, what good leffons the warie and
fkylful Readers fhall picke out of the very worft of them,
if they lift to take anie heede, and reade them not of
an intent to bee made the worfe by them, you may fee
by thefe fewe fentences, which the forefayd Sir *Thomas
Elyott* gathered as he fayth at all aduentures, intreat-
ing of the like argument. Firft *Plautus* in commendations of vertue, hath fuch like wordes.

> Verely vertue doth all thinges excell,
> For if liberty, health liuing or fubftaunce,
> Our Country our parents, and children doo well,
> It hapneth by vertue: fhe doth all aduaunce,
> Vertue hath all thinges vnder gouernaunce:
> And in whom of vertue is founde great plenty,
> Any thing that is good may neuer be dainty.

Terence, in *Eunucho* hath a profitable fpeeche, in
blafing foorth the fafhions of harlots, before the eyes
of young men. Thus fayth *Parmeno.*

> In thys thing I tryumphe in myne owne conceite,
> That I haue found for all young men the way,
> Howe they of Harlots fhall know the deceite,
> Their witts and manners: that thereby they may
> Them perpetuallie hate, for fo much as they

Out of their owne houfes be frefh and delicate,
Feeding curioufly: at home all day
Lyuing beggerlie in moft wretched eftate.

And many more wordes of the fame matter, but
which may be gathered by thefe fewe.

Ouid, in his moft wanton Bookes of loue, and the
remedies thereof, hath very many pithie and wife fentences, which a heedefull Reader may marke, and chofe
out from ye other ftuffe. This is one.

Tyme is a medicine of it fhall profitt,
VVine gyuen out of tyme may be annoyaunce.
And man fhall irritat vice if he prohibitt,
VVhen time is not meete vnto his vtteraunce.
Therfore if thou yet by counfayle art recuperable,
Fly thou from idlenes and euer be ftable.

Martiall, a moft diffolute wryter among all other,
yet not without many graue and prudent fpeeches, as
this is one worthy to be marked of thefe fond youthes
which intangle theyr wytts in raging loue, who ftepping
once ouer fhoes in theyr fancyes, neuer reft plunging
till they be ouer head and eares in their follie.

If thou wylt efchewe bitter aduenture,
And auoyde the annoyance of a penfifull hart,
Set in no one perfon all wholly thy pleafure,
The leffe maift thou ioy, but the leffe fhalt thou fmart.

Thefe are but fewe gathered out by happe, yet fufficient to fhewe that the wife and circumfpect Readers
may finde very many profitable leffons, difperfed in
thefe workes, neither take any harme by reading fuch
Poemes, but good, if they wil themfelues. Neuerthe-
les, I would not be thought to hold opinion, that the
reading of them is fo tollerable, as that there neede no
refpect to be had in making choyfe of readers or
hearers : for if they be prohibited from the tender and
vnconftant wits of children and young mindes, I thinke

it not without great reafon : neyther am I of that
deuiliifh opinion, of which fome there are, and haue
beene in England, who hauing charge of youth to in-
ftruct them in learning, haue efpecially made choyfe of
fuch vnchildifh ftuffe, to reade vnto young Schollers,
as it fhoulde feeme of fome filthy purpofe, wylfully to
corrupt theyr tender mindes, and prepare them the
more ready for theyr loathfome dyetts.

For as it is fayd of that impudent worke of *Luciane*,
a man were better to reade none of it then all of it, fo
thinke I that thefe workes are rather to be kept altogether from children, then they fhould haue free liberty
to reade them, before they be meete either of their
owne difcretion or by heedefull inftruction, to make
choyfe of the good from the badde. As for our
Englifhe Poetrie, I know no fuch perilous peeces
(except a fewe balde ditties made ouer the Beere potts,
which are nothing leffe then Poetry) which anie man
may vfe and reade without damage or daunger : which
indeede is leffe to be meruailed at among vs, then
among the olde Latines and Greekes, confidering
that Chriftianity may be a ftaie to fuch illecibrous
workes and inuentions, as among them (for their Arte
fake) myght obtaine paffage.

Nowe will I fpeake fomewhat, of that princelie part
of Poetrie, wherein are difplaied the noble actes and
valiant exploits of puiffaunt Captaines, expert fouldiers,
wife men, with the famous reportes of auncient times,
fuch as are the Heroycall workes of *Homer* in Greeke,
and the heauenly verfe of *Virgils Æneidos* in Latine :
which workes, comprehending as it were the fumme
and ground of all Poetrie, are verelie and incompar-
ably the beft of all other. To thefe, though wee haue
no Englifh worke aunfwerable, in refpect of the glorious
ornaments of gallant handling : yet our auncient Chroni-
clers and reporters of our Countrey affayres, come
moft neere them : and no doubt, if fuch regarde of
our Englifh fpeeche, and curious handling of our verfe,
had beene long fince thought vppon, and from time to

time been pollifhed and bettered by men of learning,
iudgement, and authority, it would ere this, haue
matched them in all refpects.   A manifeſt example
thereof, may bee the great good grace and fweete vayne,
which Eloquence hath attained in our fpeeche, becaufe it hath had the helpe of fuch rare and finguler
wits, as from time to time myght ſtill adde fome
amendment to the fame.   Among whom I thinke
there is none that will gainfay, but Maſter *Iohn Lilly*
hath deferued moſte high commendations, as he which
hath ſtept one ſteppe further therein then any either
before or fince he fiiſt began the wyttie difcourfe of
his *Euphues*.   Whofe workes, furely in refpecte of his
finguler eloquence and braue compofition of apt words
and fentences, let the learned examine and make tryall
thereof thorough all the partes of Rethoricke, in fitte
phrafes, in pithy fentences, in gallant tropes, in flowing
fpeeche, in plaine fence, and furely in my iudgment, I
thinke he wyll yeelde him that verdict, which *Quintilian*
giueth of bothe the beſt Orators *Demoſthenes* and
Tully, that from the one, nothing may be taken away,
to the other, nothing may be added.   But a more
neerer example to prooue my former affertion true (I
meane ye meetneffe of our fpeeche to receiue the beſt
forme of Poetry) may bee taken by conference of that
famous tranſlation of Maſter D. *Phaer* with the coppie
it felfe, who foeuer pleafe with courteous iudgement but
a little to compare and marke them both together : and
weigh with himfelfe, whether the Englifh tongue might
by little and little be brought to the verye maiefty of a
ryght Heroicall verfe.   Firſt you may marke, how *Virgill*
alwayes fitteth his matter in hande with wordes agreeable vnto the fame affection, which he expreffeth, as in
hys Tragicall exclamations, what pathe[ti]call fpeeches
he frameth ? in his comfortable confolations, howe
fmoothely hys verfe runnes ? in his dreadfull battayles,
and dreery byckerments of warres, howe bygge and
boyftrous his wordes found ? and the like notes in all
partes of his worke may be obferued.   Which excellent

grace and comely kind of choyfe, if the tranflatour hath
not hitte very neere in our courfe Englifh phrafe iudge
vprightly: wee wyll conferre fome of the places, not
picked out for the purpofe, but fuch as I tooke turning
ouer the Booke at randon. When the Troyans were
fo toft about in tempeftious wether, caufed by *Æolus*
at *Iunoes* requeft, and driuen vpon the coafte of *Affrick*
with a very neere fcape of their liues: *Æneas* after hee
had gone a land and kylled plenty of victuals for his
company of Souldiours, hee deuided the fame among
them, and thus louinglie and fweetely he comforted
them. *Æn. Lib. i.*

et dictis mærentia pectora mulcet
O focii (neque ignari fumus ante malorum)
O pafsi grauiora: dabit deus his quoque finem
Vos et fcyllæam rabiem, penitufque fonantes,
Accestis fcopulos: vos et cyclopea faxa
Experti, reuocate animos, mæftumque timorem
Mittite, forfan et hæc olim meminiffe iuuabit.
Per varios cafus, per tot difcrimina rerum
Tendimus in Latium: fedes vbi fata quietas
Ostendunt, illic fas regna refurgere troiæ.
Durate, et vofmet rebus feruate fecundis.
Talia voce refert, curifque ingentibus æger
Spem vulta fimulat, premit altum corde dolorem.

Tranflated thus.

And then to cheere their heauy harts with thefe words he
him bent.
O Mates (quoth he) that many a woe haue bidden and
borne ere thys,
Worfe haue we feene, and this alfo fhall end when Gods
wyll is.
Through *Sylla* rage (ye wott) and through the roaring
rocks we paft,
Though *Cyclops* fhore was full of feare, yet came we
through at laft.

Plucke vppe your harts, and driue from thence both
feare and care away.
To thinke on this may pleafure be perhapps another day.
By paynes and many a daunger fore, by fundry chaunce
we wend,
To come to *Italy*, where we truft to find our refting ende:
And where the deftnyes haue decreed *Troyes* Kingdome
eft to ryfe
Be bold and harden now your harts, take eafe while eafe
applies
Thus fpake he tho, but in his hart huge cares had him
oppreft,
Diffembling hope with outward eyes full heauy was his
breft.

Againe, marke the wounding of *Dido* in loue with
Æneas, with howe choyfe wordes it is pithily defcribed,
both by the Poet and the tranflator in the beginning
of the fourth booke.

At Regina graui iam dudum faucia cura

Volnus alii venis, et cæco carpitur igni, etc.

By this time perced fatte the Queene fo fore with loues
defire,
Her wound in euery vayne fhe feedes, fhe fryes in
fecrete fire.
The manhood of the man full oft, full oft his famous lyne
She doth reuolue, and from her thought his face cannot
vntwyne.
His countnaunce deepe fhe drawes and fixed faft fhe
beares in breft,
His words alfo, nor to her carefull hart can come no reft.

And in many places of the fourth booke is the fame matter fo gallantly profecuted in fweete wordes, as in mine
opinion the coppy it felfe goeth no whit beyond it.
  Compare them likewife in the woefull and lamentable

cryes of the Queene for the departure of *Æneas*, towards the ende of that Booke.

Terque quaterque manu pectus percuffa decorum

Fiauentifque abfciffa comas, proh Iupiter, ibit ?

Hic ait, et nostris inluferit aduena Regnis ? etc.

Three times her hands fhe bet, and three times ftrake her
    comely breft,
Her golden hayre fhe tare and frantiklike with moode
    oppreft,
She cryde, O *Iupiter*, O God, quoth fhe, and fhall a goe?
Indeede? and fhall a flowte me thus within my king-
    dome fo?
Shall not mine Annies out, and all my people them purfue?
Shall they not fpoyle their fhyps and burne them vp with
    vengance due?
Out people, out vppon them, follow faft with fires and
    flames,
Set fayles aloft, make out with oares, in fhips, in boates,
    in frames.
What fpeake I? or where am I? what furies me doo
    thus inchaunt?
O *Dydo*, wofull wretch, now deftnyes fell thy head
    dooth haunt.

And a little after preparing to kyll her owne felfe.

But *Dydo* quaking fierce with frantike moode and
    griefly hewe.
With trembling fpotted cheekes, her huge attempting
    to perfue.
Befides her felfe for rage, and towards death with
    vifage wanne,
Her eyes about fhe rolde, as redde as blood they
    looked than.

At laft ready to fall vppon *Æneas* fworde.

O happy (welaway) and ouer happy had I beene,
If neuer Troian fhyps (ahlas) my Country fhore had feene.
Thus fayd fhe wryde her head, and vnreuenged muft
    we die ?
But let vs boldly die (quoth fhee) thus, thus to death
    I ply.

Nowe likewife for the braue warlike phrafe and bygge
founding kynd of thundring fpeeche, in the hotte fkyr-
myfhes of battels, you may confer them in any of the
laft fiue Bookes: for examples fake, thys is one about
the ninth Booke.

> *Et clamor totis per propugnacula muris,*
> *Intendunt acries arcus, amentaque torquent.*
> *Sternitur omne folum telis, tum fcutæ cauæque*
> *Dant fonitum flictu galeæ: pugna asper furgit?* *etc.*

A clamarous noyfe vpmounts on fortreffe tops and
    bulwarks towres,
They ftrike, they bend their bowes, they whirle from
    ftrings fharp fhoting fhowres.
All ftreetes with tooles are ftrowed, than helmets,
    fkulles, with battrings marrd.
And fhieldes difhyuering cracke, vprifeth roughneffe
    byckring hard
Looke how the tempeft ftorme when wind out wraft-
    ling blowes at fouth,
Raine ratling beates the grownde, or clowdes of haile
    from Winters mouth,
Downe dafhyng headlong driues, when God from fkyes
    with griefly fteuen,
His watry fhowres outwrings, and whirlwind clowdes
    downe breakes from heauen.

And fo foorth much more of the like effect.

Onely one comparifon more will I defire you to marke
at your leyfures, which may ferue for all the reft, that
is, the defcription of Fame, as it is in the 4. booke,
towardes the end, of which it followeth thus.

*Monstrum horrendum ingens cui quot funt corpore plumæ
Tot vigilos oculi etc.*

Monfter gaftly great, for euery plume her carkaffe beares,
Like number learing eyes fhe hath, like number
    harkning eares,
Like number tongues, and mouthes fhe wagges, a
    wondrous thing to fpeake,
At midnight foorth fhee flyes, and vnder fhade her
    found dooth fqueake.
All night fhe wakes, nor flumber fweete doth take nor
    neuer fleepes.
By dayes on houfes tops fhee fits or gates of Townes
    fhe keepes.
On watching Towres fhe clymbes, and Citties great .
    fhe makes agaft,
Both trueth and falfhood forth fhe telles, and lyes
    abroade doth caft.

But what neede I to repeate any more places? there
is not one Booke among the twelue, which wyll not
yeelde you moft excellent pleafure in conferring the
tranflation with the Coppie, and marking the gallant
grace which our Englifhe fpeeche affoordeth. And in
trueth the like comparifons, may you choofe out
through the whole tranflations of the *Metamorphofis* by
Mafter *Golding* who (confidering both their Coppyes)
hath equally deferued commendations for the beautifying of the Englifh fpeeche. It would be tedious
to ftay to rehearfe any places out of him nowe: let
the other fuffice to prooue, that the Englifh tongue
lacketh neyther variety nor currantneffe of phrafe for
any matter.

 Wyll nowe fpeake a little of an other kinde of poetical writing, which might notwith-ftanding for the variableneffe of the argu-ment therein vfually handled, bee com-prehended in thofe kindes before declared: that is, the compyling *Eglogues,* as much to fay as Goteheardes tales, becaufe they bee commonly Dia-logues or fpeeches framed or fuppofed betweene Sheepeheardes, Neteheardes, Goteheardes, or fuch like fimple men: in which kind of writing, many haue obtained as immortall prayfe and commendation, as in any other.

The cheefeft of thefe is *Theocritus* in Greeke, next him, and almoft the very fame, is *Virgill* in Latin. After *Virgyl* in like fort writ *Titus Calphurnius* and *Baptifta Mantuan,* wyth many other both in Latine and other languages very learnedlye. Although the matter they take in hand feemeth commonlie in ap-pearaunce rude and homely, as the vfuall talke of fimple clownes: yet doo they indeede vtter in the fame much pleafaunt and profitable delight. For vnder thefe perfonnes, as it were in a cloake of fimpli-citie, they would eyther fette foorth the prayfes of theyr freendes, without the note of flattery, or enueigh grieuoufly againft abufes, without any token of byt-terneffe.

Somwhat like vnto thefe works, are many peeces of *Chawcer,* but yet not altogether fo poeticall. But nowe yet at ye laft hath England hatched vppe one Poet of this forte, in my confcience comparable with the beft in any refpect: euen Mafter *Sp*: Author of the *Sheepeheardes Calender,* whofe trauell in that peece of Englifh Poetrie, I thinke verely is fo commendable, as none of equall iudgment can yeelde him leffe prayfe

for hys excellent ſkyll, and ſkylfull excellency ſhewed
foorth in the ſame, then they would to eyther *Theocritus* or *Virgill*, whom in mine opinion, if the courſe-
nes of our ſpeeche (I meane the courſe of cuſtome
which he woulde not infringe) had beene no more let
vnto him, then theyr pure natiue tongues were vnto
them, he would haue (if it might be) ſurpaſſed them.
What one thing is there in them ſo worthy admiration,
whereunto we may not adioyne ſome thing of his, of
equall deſert? Take *Virgil* and make ſome little
compariſon betweene them, and iudge as ye ſhall
ſee cauſe.

Virgill hath a gallant report of *Auguſtus* couertly
compryſed in the firſt *Æglogue*: the like is in him, of
her Maieſtie, vnder the name of *Eliza*. *Virgill* maketh
a braue coloured complaint of vnſtedfaſt freendſhyppe
in the perſon of *Corydon*: the lyke is him in his 5
Æglogue. Agayne behold the pretty Paſtorall contentions of *Virgill* in the third *Æglogue*: of him in ye
eight *Eglogue*. Finally, either in compariſon with
them, or reſpect of hys owne great learning, he may
well were the Garlande, and ſteppe before ye beſt of
all Engliſh Poets that I haue ſeene or hearde: for I
thinke no leſſe deſerueth (thus ſayth *E, K* in hys
commendations) hys wittineſſe in deuiſing, his pithi
neſſe in vttering, his complaintes of loue ſo louely, his
diſcourſes of pleaſure ſo pleaſantly, his Paſtrall rude
nes, his Morrall wyſeneſſe, his due obſeruing of *decorum*
euery where, in perſonages, in ſeaſon, in matter, in
ſpeeche, and generally in all ſeemely' ſimplicity, of
handling hys matter and framing hys wordes. The
occaſion of his worke is a warning to other young men,
who being intangled in loue and youthful vanities,
may learne to looke to themſelues in time, and to
auoyde inconueniences which may breede if they be
not in time preuented. Many good Morrall leſſons
aie therein contained, as the reuerence which young
men owe to the aged in the ſecond *Eglogue*: the
caueate or warning to beware a ſubtill profeſſor of

freendfhippe in the fift *Eglogue*: the commendation of
good Paftors, and fhame and difprayfe of idle and
ambitious Goteheardes in the feauenth, the loofe and
retchleffe lyuing of Popifh Prelates in the ninth. The
learned and fweete complaynt of the contempt of
learning vnder the name of Poetry in the tenth.
There is alfo much matter vttered fomewhat couertly,
efpecially ye abufes of fome whom he would not be
too playne withall: in which, though it be not appar-
ant to euery one, what hys fpeciall meaning was, yet
fo fkilfully is it handled, as any man may take much
delight at hys learned conueyance, and picke out
much good fence in the moft obfcureft of it. Hys
notable prayfe deferued in euery parcell of that worke,
becaufe I cannot expreffe as I woulde and as it fhould:
I wyll ceafe to fpeake any more of, the rather becaufe
I neuer hearde as yet any that hath reade it, which
hath not with much admiration commended it. One
only thing therein haue I hearde fome curious heades
call in queftion: *viz*: the motion of fome vnfauery
loue, fuch as in the fixt *Eglogue* he feemeth to deale
withall (which fay they) is fkant allowable to Englifh
eares, and might well haue beene left for the Italian
defenders of loathfome beaftlines, of whom perhappes
he learned it: to thys obiection I haue often aunfwered
and (I thinke truely) that theyr nyce opinion ouer
fhooteth the Poets meaning, who though hee in that
as in other thinges, immitateth the auncient Poets, yet
doth not meane, no more did they before hym, any
difordered loue, or the filthy luft of the deuillifh
Pederaftice taken in the worfe fence, but rather to
fhewe howe the diffolute life of young men intangled
in loue of women, doo neglect the freendfhyp and
league with their olde freendes and familiers. Why
(fay they) yet he fhold gyue no occafion of fufpition,
nor offer to the viewe of Chriftians, any token of fuch
filthineffe, howe good foeuer hys meaning were: wherevnto I oppofe the fimple conceyte they haue of matters
which concerne learning or wytt, wylling them to gyue

Poets leaue to vfe theyr vayne as they fee good: it is
their foolyfh conftruction, not hys wryting that is
blameable. Wee muft prefcrybe to no wryters, (much
leffe to Poets) in what forte they fhould vtter theyr
conceyts. But thys wyll be better difcuffed by fome
I hope of better abillity.

One other forte of Poeticall wryters remayneth yet
to bee remembred, that is, The precepts of Hufbandry,
learnedly compiled in Heroycall verfe. Such were the
workes of *Hefiodus* in *Greeke*, and *Virgils Georgickes*
in Latine. What memorable worke hath beene handled in immitation of thefe by any Englifh Poet, I know
not, (faue onely one worke of M. *Tuffer*, a peece
furely of great wytt and experience, and wythal very
prettilye handled) And I thinke the caufe why our
Poets haue not trauayled in that behalfe, is efpecially,
for that there haue beene alwayes plenty of other
wryters that haue handled the fame argument very
largely. Among whom Mafter *Barnabe Googe*, in
tranflating and enlarging the moft profitable worke of
Heresbachius, hath deferued much commendation, as
well for hys faythfull compyling and learned increafing
the noble worke, as for hys wytty tranflation of a
good part of the *Georgickes* of *Virgill* into Englifh
verfe.

Among all the tranflations, which hath beene my
fortune to fee, I could neuer yet finde that worke of
the *Georgicks* wholly performed. I remember once
Abraham Flemming in his conuerfion of the *Eglogues*,
promifed to tranflate and publifhe it: whether he dyd
or not I knowe not, but as yet I heard not of it. I
my felfe wott well I beftowed fome time in it two or
three yeeres fince, turning it to that fame Englifh verfe,
which other fuch workes were in, though it were rudely:
howe beit, I did it onely for mine owne vfe, and vppon
certayne refpectes towardes a Gentleman mine efpeciall
freende, to whom I was defirous to fhewe fome token
of duetifull good wyll, and not minding it fhould goe
farre abroade, confidering howe flenderly I ranne it

ouer, yet fince then, hath one gott it in keeping, who as it is told me, eyther hath or wyll vnaduifedly pub-lifhe it: which iniury though he meanes to doo me in myrth, yet I hope he wyll make me fome fuffycient recompence, or els I fhall goe neere to watch hym the like or a worfe turne.

But concerning the matter of our Englyfh wryters, lett thys fuffice: nowe fhall ye heare my fimple fkyl in what I am able to fay concerning the forme and manner of our Englyfhe verfe.

The moft vfuall and frequented kind of our Englifh Poetry hath alwayes runne vpon, and to this day is obferued in fuch equall number of fyllables, and like-nes of wordes, that in all places one verfe either im-mediatly, or by mutuall interpofition, may be aunfwer-able to an other both in proportion of length, and ending of lynes in the fame Letters. Which rude kinde of verfe, though (as I touched before) it rather difcrediteth our fpeeche, as borrowed from the *Bar-barians*, then furnifheth the fame with any comely ornament: yet beeing fo ingraffed by cuftome, and fre-quented by the moft parte, I may not vtterly diffalowe it, leaft I fhould feeme to call in queftion the iudge-ment of all our famous wryters, which haue wonne eternall prayfe by theyr memorable workes compyled in that verfe.

For my part therefore, I can be content to efteeme it as a thing, the perfection whereof is very commend-able, yet fo as wyth others I could wyfh it were by men of learning and ability bettered, and made more artificiall, according to the woorthines of our fpeeche.

The falling out of verfes together in one like founde, is commonly called in Englifh, Ryme, taken from the Greeke worde Pυθμος, which furely in my iudgment is verye abufiuelye applyed to fuch a fence: and by thys, the vnworthineffe of the thing may well appeare, in that wanting a proper name, wherby to be called, it borroweth a word farre exceeding the dignitye of it,

and not appropriate to fo rude or bafe a thing. For
Ryme is properly, the iuſt proportion of a claufe or
fentence, whether it be in profe or meeter, aptly com-
prifed together: wherof there is both an naturall and
an artificiall compofition, in any manner or kynde of
fpeeche, eyther French, Italian, Spanifh or Englifh:
and is propper not onely to Poets, but alfo to Readers,
Oratours, Pleaders, or any which are to pronounce or
fpeake any thing in publike audience.

The firſt begynning of Ryme (as we nowe terme it)
though it be fomewhat auncient, yet nothing famous.
In Greece (they fay) one *Symias Rhodias*, becaufe he
would be finguler in fomthing, wryt poetically of the
Fable, contayning howe *Iupiter* beeing in fhape of a
Swanne, begatte the Egge on Leda, wherof came
Caſtor, Pollux, and Helena, whereof euery verfe ended
in thys Ryme, and was called therefore ὠον but thys
foolyfhe attempt was fo contemned and difpyfed,
that the people would neither admitte the Author nor -
Booke any place in memory of learning. Since that
it was not hearde of, till ye time ye *Hunnes* and
Gothians renued it agayne, and brought it into Italie.
But howfoeuer or wherefoeuer it beganne, certayne it
is, that in our Englifh tongue it beareth as good grace,
or rather better, then in any other: and is a faculty
whereby many may and doo deferue great prayfe and
commendation, though our fpeeche be capable of a
farre more learned manner of verfifying, as I wyl partly
declare heereafter.

There be three fpeciall notes neceffary to be obferued
in the framing of our accuſtomed Englifh Ryme: the
firſt is, that one meeter or verfe be aunfwerable to an
other, in equall number of feete or fyllables, or pro-
portionable to the tune whereby it is to be reade or
meafured. The feconde, to place the words in fuch
forte, as none of them be wreſted contrary to the
naturall inclination or affectation of the fame, or more
truely ye true quantity thereof. The thyrd, to make
them fall together mutually in Ryme, that is, in wordes

of like founde, but fo as the wordes be not difordered for the Rymes fake, nor the fence hindered. Thefe be the moſt pryncipall obſeruations, which I thinke requifite in an Englifh verſe: for as for the other ornaments which belong thereto, they be more properly belonging to the feuerall gyfts of ſkylfull Poets, then common notes to be preſcribed by me: but fomewhat perhaps I fhall haue occafion to fpeake heereafter.

Of the kyndes of Englifh verſes which differ in number of fyllables, there are almoſt infinite: which euery way alter according to hys fancy, or to the meafure of that meeter, wherein it pleafeth hym to frame hys ditty. Of the beſt and moſt frequented I wyll rehearfe fome. The longeſt verfe in length, which I haue feene vfed in Englifh confiſteth of fix-teene fyllables, eache two verfes ryming together, thus.

Wher vertue wants and vice abounds, there wealth is but a bayted hooke,
To make men fwallow down their bane, before on danger deepe they looke.

Thys kynde is not very much vfed at length thus, but is commonly deuided, eche verfe into two, whereof eche fhal containe eyght fyllables, and ryme croffe wyfe, the firſt to the thyrd, and the fecond to the fourth, in this manner.

> Great wealth is but a bayted hooke.
> VVhere vertue wants, and vice aboundes:
> VVhich men deuoure before they looke,   ·
> So them in daungers deepe it drownes.

An other kynd next in length to thys, is, where eche verfe hath fourteene fyllables, which is the moſt ac-cuſtomed of all other, and efpecially vfed of all the tranſlatours of the Latine Poets for the moſt part thus.

My mind with furye fierce inflamde of late I know not howe,
Doth burne Parnaffus hyll to fee, adornd wyth Lawrell bowe.

Which may likewyfe and fo it often is deuyded. eche

verfe into two, to [the?] firft hauing eyght fillables, the
fecond fixe, wherof the two fixes fhall alwayes ryme,
and fometimes the eyghtes, fometimes not, according
to the wyll of the maker.

> My minde with furye fierce inflamde,
> Of late I knowe not howe :
> Doth burne *Pernaffus* hyll to fee,
> Adornd wyth Lawrell bowe.

There are nowe wythin this compaffe, as many fortes
of verfes as may be deuifed differences of numbers:
wherof fome confift of equall proportions, fome of long
and fhort together, fome of many rymes in one ftaffe
(as they call it) fome of croffe ryme, fome of counter
ryme, fome ryming wyth one worde farre diftant from
another, fome ryming euery thyrd or fourth word, and
fo likewyfe all manner of dytties applyable to euery
tune that may be fung or fayd, diftinct from profe or
continued fpeeche. To auoyde therefore tedioufneffe
and confufion, I wyll repeate onely the different fortes
of verfes out of the *Sheepeheardes Calender*, which
may well ferue to beare authoritie in thys matter.

There are in that worke twelue or thirteene fundry
forts of verfes, which differ eyther in length, or ryme,
of deftinction of the ftaues: but of them which differ
in length or number of fillables not paft fixe or feauen.
The firft of them is of tenne fillables, or rather fiue
feete in one verfe, thus,

> A Sheepheards boy no better doo him call,
> When Winters waftfull fpight was almoft fpent.

This verfe he vfeth commonly in hys fweete com-
playntes, and mornefull ditties, as very agreeable to
fuch affections.

The fecond fort hath naturally but nyne fyllables,
and is a more rough or clownifh manner of verfe, vfed
moft commonly of him if you mark him in hys

fatyricall reprehenfions, and his Sheepeheardes home·
lyeſt talke, ſuch as the ſecond *Æglogue* is.

> Ah for pitty wyll rancke Winters rage,
> Theſe bytter blaſts neuer gynne to aſſwage.

The number of nine ſillables in thys verſe is very often
altered, and ſo it may without any difgrace to the
ſame, efpecially where the ſpeeche ſhould be moſt
clowniſh and ſimple, which is much obferued of hym.

The third kynd is a pretty rounde verſe, running
currantly together, commonly feauen ſillables or ſometime eyght in one verſe, as many in the next, both
ryming together: euery two hauing one the like verſe
after them, but of rounder wordes, and two of them
likewyſe ryming mutually. That verſe expreſſeth
notably, light and youthfull talke, ſuch as is the
thyrde *Æglogue* betweene two Sheepheardes boys
concerning loue.

> *Thomalin* why ſitten we ſo
> As weren ouerwent with woe
> Vpon ſo fayre a morrowe?
> The ioyous time now nigheth faſt
> That wyll allay this bitter blaſt
> And ſlake the Winter ſorrow.

The fourth ſort containeth in eche ſtaffe manie
vnequall verſes, but moſt ſweetelie falling together.
which the Poet calleth the tune of the waters fall.
Therein is his ſong In prayſe of *Eliza.*

> Ye daintie Nymphes which in this bleſſed brooke
>   doo bathe your breſt,
> Forſake your watrie bowres and hether looke,
>   at my requeſt.
> And eke yee Virgins that on *Parnaſs* dwell,
> Whence floweth *Helicon* the learned Well,
>   helpe me to blaze
>   her woorthy praiſe
> That in her ſex doth all excell. etc.

The fift, is a deuided verfe of twelue fillables into
two verfes, whereof I fpake before, and feemeth moft
meete for ye handling of a Morrall matter, fuch as is
the praife of good Paftors, and the difpraife of ill in
the feauenth *Æglogue.*

The fixt kinde, is called a round, beeing mutuallie
fung betweene two: one fingeth one verfe, the other
the next, eche rymeth with himfelfe.

> **Per.** It fell vppon a holie eue
> **Wpl.** Hey ho holliday
> **Per.** When holie fathers wont to fhrieue,
> **Wpl.** Thus ginneth our Rondelay. etc.

The feauenth forte is a verie tragicall mournefull
meafure, wherein he bewayleth the death of fome
freend vnder the perfon of *Dydo.*

> Vp then *Melpomene* the mournfulft Mufe of nyne,
>   fuch caufe of mourning neuer hadft afore:
> Vp griefly ghoftes, and vp my mournfull ryme:
>   matter of myrth now fhalt thou haue no more.
>   *Dydo* my deere alas is dead,
>   Dead and lyeth wrapt in leade:
>   O heauie hearfe
>   Let ftreaming teares be powred out in ftore
>   O carefull vearfe.

Thefe fortes of verfes for breuities fake haue I chofen
foorth of him, whereby I fhall auoide the tedious rehearfall of all the kindes which are vfed: which I
thinke would haue beene vnpoffible, feeing they may
be altered to as manie formes as the Poets pleafe:
neither is there anie tune or ftroke which may be fung
or plaide on inftruments, which hath not fome poetical
ditties framed according to the numbers thereof: fome
to Rogero, fome to Trenchmore, to downe right Squire,
to Galliardes, to Pauines, to Iygges, to Brawles, to all
manner of tunes which euerie Fidler knowes better
then my felfe, and therefore I will let them paffe.

Againe, the diuerfities of the ftaues (which are the number of verfes contained with the diuifions or partitions of a ditty) doo often times make great differences in thefe verfes. As when one ftaffe containeth but two verfes, or (if they bee deuided) foure: the firft or the firft couple hauing twelue fillables, the other fourteene, which verfifyers call Powlters meafure, becaufe fo they tall[i]e their wares by dozens. Alfo, when one ftaffe hath manie verfes, whereof eche one rimeth to the next, or mutuallie croffe, or diftant by three, or by foure, or ended contrarye to the beginning, and a hundred fortes, whereof to fhewe feuerall examples, would bee too troublefome: nowe for the fecond point.

The naturall courfe of moft Englifh verfes feemeth to run vppon the olde Iambicke ftroake, and I may well thinke by all likelihoode, it had the beginning thereof. For if you marke the right quantitie of our vfuall verfes, ye fhall perceiue them to containe in found ye very propertie of Iambick feete, as thus.

◡ — ◡ — ◡ — ◡ — ◡ — ◡ — ◡ —
I that my flender oaten pipe in verfe was wont to founde:

For tranfpofe anie of thofe feete in pronouncing, and make fhort either the two, foure, fixe, eight, tenne, twelue fillable, and it will (doo what you can) fall out very abfurdly.

Againe, though our wordes can not well bee forced to abyde the touch of *Pofition* and other rules of *Profodia*, yet is there fuch a naturall force or quantity in eche worde, that it will not abide anie place but one, • without fome foule difgrace: as for example try anie verfe, as thys,

◡ — ◡ — ◡ — ◡ — ◡ — ◡ — ◡ —
Of fhapes tranfformde to bodies ftrange I purpofe to intreate.

Make the firft fillable long, or the third, or the fift and fo foorth: or contrariwife make the other fillables to admitte the fhortneffe of one of them places, and fee

what a wonderfull defacing it wil be to the wordes, as
thus.

— ᴜ — ᴜ — ᴜ — ᴜ — ᴜ —ᴜ — ᴜ
Of ftrange bodies tranfformd to fhapes purpofe I to intreat.

So that this is one efpeciall thing to be taken heede of
in making a good Englifh verfe, that by difplacing no
worde bee wrefted againft his naturall propriety, wherevnto you fhal perceyue eche worde to be affected, and
may eafilie difcerne it in wordes of two fillables or aboue,
though fome there be of indifferencie, that wyll ftand
in any place. Againe, in chouching the whole fentence,
the like regarde is to be had, that wee exceede not too
boldly in placing the verbe out of his order, and too
farre behinde the nowne: which the neceffitie of Ryme
may oftentimes vrge. For though it be tollerable in
a verfe to fette wordes fo extraordinarily as other
fpeeche will not admitt, yet heede is to be taken, leaft
by too much affecting that manner, we make both the
verfe vnpleafant and the fence obfcure. And fure it ir
a wonder to fee the folly of manie in this refpect, that
vfe not onely too much of thys ouerthwart placing, or
rather difplacing of wordes, in theyr Poemes and verfes,
but alfo in theyr profe or continued writings: where
they thinke to rolle moft fmoothlie, and flow moft
eloquently, there by this means, come foorth theyr
fentences dragging at one Authors tayle as they were
tyde together with poynts, where often you fhall tarrie
(fcratching your heade) a good fpace before you fhall
heare hys principall verbe or fpeciall word, leafte hys
finging grace, which in his fentence is contained fhould
be leffe, and his fpeeche feeme nothing poeticall.
The thyrd obferuation is, the Ryme or like ending
of verfes: which though it is of leaft importance, yet
hath won fuch credite among vs, that of all other it is
moft regarded of the greateft part of Readers. And
furely as I am perfwaded, the regarde of wryters to this,
hath beene the greateft decay of that good order of
verfifying, which might ere this haue beene eftablifhed

in our fpeeche. In my iudgment, if there be any ornament in the fame, it is rather to be attributed to the
plentifull fulneffe of our fpeeche, which can affoorde
ryming words fufficient for the handling of any matter,
then to the thing it felfe for any beautifying it bringeth
to a worke: which might bee adorned with farre more
excellent collours then ryming is.   Notwithftanding I
cannot but yeelde vnto it (as cuftome requireth) the
deferued prayfes, efpecially where it is with good iudgement ordered.   And I thinke them right worthy of
admiration, for their readines and plenty of wytt and
capacity, who can with facility intreate at large, and
as we call it *extempore*, in good and feucible ryme,
vppon fome vnacquainted matter.

   The ready fkyll of framing anie thing in verfe, befides
the naturall promptneffe which many haue therevnto,
is much helped by Arte, and exercife of the memory:
for as I remember, I reade one among *Gaskoynes*
workes, a little inftruction to verfifying, where is prefcribed as I thinke thys courfe of learning to verfifye
in Ryme.

   When ye haue one verfe well fetled, and decently
ordered which you may difpofe at your pleafure, to
ende it with what word you wyll: then what foeuer the
word is, you may fpeedilie runne ouer the other wordes
which are aunfwerable therevnto, (for more readines
through all the letters Alphabetically) whereof you may
choofe that which wyll beft fitte the fence of your matter
in that place: as for example: if your laft worde ende
in Booke, you may ftraightwayes in your minde runne
them ouer thus.   Brooke, Cooke, crooke, hooke, looke,
nooke, pooke, rooke, forfooke, tooke, awooke etc.
Nowe it is twenty to one, but alwayes one of thefe fhall
iumpe with your former worde and matter in good
fence.   If not, then alter the firft.

   And indeede I thinke, that next to the Arte of
memory, thys is the readyeft way to attaine to the
faculty of ryming well Extempore, efpecially if it be
helped with thus much paynes.   Gather together all

manner of wordes efpecially *Monafillables*, and place
them Alphabetically in fome note, and either haue
them meetely perfectly by hart (which is no verye
labourfome matter) or but looke them dilligently ouer
at fome time, practifing to ryme indifferent often,
whereby I am perfwaded it wil foone be learned, fo as
the party haue withall any reafonable gyft of knowledge
and learning, whereby hee want not bothe matter and
wordes altogether.

What the other circumftaunces of Ryming are, as
what wordes may tollerably be placed in Ryme, and
what not: what words doo beft become a Ryme, and
what not, how many fortes of Ryme there is: and fuch
like I wyll not ftay nowe to intreate. There be many
more obferuations and notes to be prefcribed, to the
exacte knowledge of verfifying, which I truft wilbe
better and larger laide forth by others, to whom I de-
ferre manie confiderations in this treatife: hoping that
fome of greater fkill will fhortlie handle this matter in
better forte.

Nowe the fundry kindes of rare deuifes, and pretty
inuentions which come from ye fine poeticall vaine of
manie in ftrange and vnacuftomed manner, if I could
report them, it were worthie my trauell: fuch are the
turning of verfes: the infolding of wordes: the fine
repititions: the clarklie conueying of contraries, and
manie fuch like. Whereof though I coulde fette downe
manie: yet becaufe I want bothe manie and the beft
kindes of them, I will ouerpaffe: onelie pointing you
to one or two which may fuffice for example.

Looke vppon the rufull fong of *Colin* fung by
Cuddie in the *Sheepheardes Calender*, where you fhall
fee a finguler rare deuife of a dittie framed vpon thefe
fixe wordes *V Voe, founde, cryes, paft, fleep, augment*,
which are moft prettilie turned and wounde vppe
mutually together, expreffing wonderfully the doleful-
neffe of the fong. A deuife not much vnlike vnto the
fame, is vfed by fome, who taking the laft wordes of a
certaine number of verfes as it were by the rebound

of an *Echo*, fhall make them fall out in fome prettie
fence.

Of this forte there are fome deuifed by *Iohn Graunge*,
which becaufe they be not long I wyll rehearfe one.

> If feare oppreffe howe then may hope me fhielde?
> Denyall fayes, vayne hope hath pleafed well,
> But as fuch hope thou wouldeft not be thine,
> So would I not the like to rule my hart.
> For if thou loueft it bidds thee graunt forthwith
> Which is the ioy whereof I liue in hope.

Here if you take the laft worde of euerie verfe, and
place them orderlie together, you fhall haue this fentence: *Shielde well thyne hart with hope.* But of
thefe *Echoes* I knowe indeede verie daintie peeces of
worke, among fome of the fineft Poets this day in London: who for the rareneffe of them keepe them priuelie
to themfelues, and wil not let them come abroad.

A like inuention to the laft rehearfed, or rather a
better, haue I feene often practifed in framing a whole
dittie to the Letters of ones name, or to the wordes of
fome two or three verfes which is very witty, as for
example this is one of *W. Hunnis*, which for the
fhortnes I rather chufde then fome yat are better.

> If thou defire to liue in quiet reft,
> Gyue eare and fee, but fay the beft.

Thefe two verfes are nowe as it were refolued into
dyuers other, euery two wordes or fillables being the
beginning of an other like verfe, in this fort.

If thou ⎧delight in quietnes of life,
Defire ⎪to fhunne from brawles, debate and ftrife:
To liue ⎨in loue with G O D, with freend and foe,
In reft ⎩fhalt fleepe when other cannot fo.

Gyue eare ⎧to all, yet doo not all beleeue,
And fee ⎪the end and then thy fentence gyue:
But fay ⎨For trueth of happy liues affignde
The beft ⎩hath he that quiet is in minde.

Thus are there infinite fortes of fine conueiances (as
they may be termed) to be vfed, and are much frequented by verfifyers, as well in compofition of their
verfe, as the wittines of their matter : which all I will
referre to the confideration of euerie pleafant headded
Poet in their proper gifts : onelie I fett downe thefe
fewe fortes of their formes of verfifying, which may
ftand in fteede to declare what manie others may be
deuifed in like forte.

But nowe to proceede to the reformed kind of Englifh verfe which manie haue before this, attempted to
put in practife, and to eftablifh for an accuftomed right
among Englifh Poets, you fhall heare in like manner
my fimple iudgment concerning the fame.

I am fully and certainlie perfwaded, that if the true
kind of verfifying in immitation of Greekes and Latines,
had beene practifed in the Englifh tongue, and put in
vre from time to tyme by our Poets, who might haue
continually beene mending and pollyfhing the fame,
euery one according to their feuerall giftes : it would
long ere this haue afpyred to as full perfection, as in
anie other tongue whatfoeuer.   For why may I not
thinke fo of our Englifh, feeing that among the
Romaines a long time, yea euen till the dayes of
Tully, they efteemed not the Latine Poetrie almoft
worth any thing, iñ refpecte of the Greeke, as appeareth in the Oration *pro Archia Poeta* : yet afterwardes
it increafed in credite more and more, and that in
fhort fpace : fo that in *Virgilles* time, wherein were
they not comparable with the Greekes ?   So likewife,
now it feemeth not currant for an Englifh verfe to runne
vpon true quantity, and thofe feete which the Latines
vfe, becaufe it is ftraunge, and the other barbarous
cuftome, beeing within compaffe of euery bafe witt,
hath worne it out of credite or eftimation.   But if our
wryters, beeing of learning and iudgment, would rather
infringe thys curious cuftome, then omitte the occafion
of inlarging the credite of their natiue fpeeche, and
theyr owne prayfes, by practifing that commendable

kind of wryting in true verfe : then no doubt, as in
other partes of learning, fo in Poetry, fhoulde not
ftoupe to the beft of them all in all maner of ornament and comlineffe.   But fome obiect that our
wordes are nothing refemblaunt in nature to theirs,
and therefore not poffible to bee framed with any good
grace after their vfe : but cannot we then as well as the
Latines did, alter the cannon of the rule according to
the quality of our worde, and where our wordes and
theyrs wyll agree, there to iumpe with them, where
they will not agree, there to eftablifh a rule of our
owne to be directed by ?   Likewife, for ye tenor of
the verfe might we not (as *Horace* dyd in the Latine)
alter their proportions to what fortes we lifted, and to
what we fawe wold beft become the nature of the
thing handled, or the quallity of the words ?   Surely
it is to be thought that if any one, of found iudgment
and learning, fhoulde putt foorth fome famous worke,
contayning dyuers formes of true verfes, fitting the
meafures, according to the matter : it would of it felfe
be a fufficient authority without any prefcription of
rules, to the moft part of Poets, for them to follow and
by cuftome to ratify.   For fure it is, that the rules and
principles of Poetry, were not precifely followed and
obferued of the firft beginners and wryters of Poetry,
but were felected and gathered feuerally out of theyr
workes, for the direction and behoofe of their followers.
And indeede, he that fhall with heedefull iudgment
make tryall of the Englifh wordes, fhall not finde them
fo groffe or vnapt, but that they wyll become any one
of ye moft accuftomed fortes of Latine or Greeke
verfes meetely, and run thereon fomewhat currantly.

I my felfe, with fimple fkyll I confeffe, and farre
vnable iudgment, haue ventured on a fewe, which notwithftanding the rudenes of them may ferue to fhewe
what better might bee brought into our fpeeche, if thofe
which are of meete abilitye woulde beftowe fome trauell
and endeuour thereuppon.   But before I fette them
downe, I wyll fpeake fomewhat of fuch obferuations as

I could gather neceſſary to the knowledge of thefe
kinde of verfes, leaſt I fhould feeme to runne vpon
them rafhly, without regarde either of example or
authority.

The fpeciall poyntes of a true verfe, are the due
obferuations of the feete, and place of the feete.

The foote of a verfe, is a meafure of two fillables, or
of three, diſtinguifhed by time which is eyther long or
fhort. A foote of two fillables, is eyther fimple or
mixt, that is, of like time or of diuers. A fimple foote of
two fillables is likewife twofolde, eyther of two long
fillables called *Spondæus*, as – – *goodneſſe*, or of two
fhort called *Pyrrichius* as ᴗ ᴗ *hyther*. A myxt foote of
2. fillables, is eyther of one fhort and one long called
Iambus as ᴗ – *dying*: or of one long and one fhort,
called *Choreus* as – ᴗ *gladly*. A foote of 3. fillables
in like forte is either fimple or myxt. The fimple is
eyther *Moloſſus*, that is of three long, as – – – *forgiue-
nes*: or *Trochæus*, that is of 3. fhort, as ᴗ ᴗ ᴗ *merylie*.
The mixt is of 6. diuers fortes, 1. *Daƈylus*, of one long,
and two fhort, as – ᴗ ᴗ *happily*. 2. *Anapætus*, of two
fhorte, and one long, as ᴗ ᴗ – *t[r]auelers*. 3. *Bacchius*,
of one fhort, and two long, as ᴗ – – *remembrers*.
4. *Palimbachius*, of two long and one fhort, as – – ᴗ
accorded. 5. *Creticus* of a long, a fhort, and a long,
– ᴗ – *daungerous*. 6. *Amphibrachus*, of a fhort, a long,
and a fhort, as ᴗ – ᴗ *reioyced*.

Many more deuifions of feete are vfed by fome, but
thefe doo more artificially comprehende all quantities
neceſſary to the fkanning of any verfe, according to
Tallæus in hys Rethorique. The place of the feete is
the difpofing of them in theyr propper roomes, whereby
may be difcerned the difference of eche verfe which is
the right numbring of the fame. Now as for the quantity of our wordes, therein lyeth great difficultye, and the
cheefeſt matter in this faculty. For in truth there being
fuch diuerfity betwixt our words and the Latine, it
cannot ſtande indeede with great reafon that they
fhoulde frame, wee beeing onelie directed by fuch rules

as ferue for onely Latine words, yet notwithftanding
one may well perceiue by thefe fewe, that thefe kinde
of verfes would well become the fpeeche, if fo bee there
were fuch Rules prefcribed, as woulde admitt the placing of your apteft and fulleft wordes together.   For
indeede excepting a fewe, of our *Monafyllables*, which
naturally fhoulde moft of them be long, we haue almoft
none, that wyll ftande fitlie in a fhort foote: and therfore if fome exception were made againft the precife
obferuation of *Pofition*, and certaine other of the rules,
then might we haue as great plenty and choyfe of good
woordes to furnifh and fette foorth a verfe, as in any
other tongue.

Likewife if there were fome derection in fuch wordes,
as fall not within the compaffe of Greeke or Latine
rules, it were a great helpe, and therefore I had great
miffe in thefe few which I made.   Such as is the laft
fillable in thefe wordes, *able*, *noble*, or *poffible* and
fuch like: againe for the nature and force of our *W*. of
our *th*, of our *oo*, and *ee*, of our wordes which admytte
an *e* in the ende after one or two Confonantes, and
many other.   I for my part, though (I muft needes
confeffe) many faultes efcaped me in thefe fewe, yet
tooke I as good heede as I coulde, and in trueth did
rather alwaies omitt the beft wordes and fuch as would
naturally become the fpeech beft, then I wolde committe any thing, which fhoulde notorioufly impugne the
Latine rules, which herein I had onely for my direction.
Indeede moft of our *Monafyllables* I am forced to make
fhort, to fupply the want of many fhort wordes requifite
in thefe verfes.   The Participle *A*, being but the Englifh article adioyned to Nownes, I alwayes make fhort,
both alone and in compofition, and likewife the wordes
of one fillable ending in *E*, as *the*, when it is an article,
he, *fhe*, *ye*, etc. *we* I thinke fhould needes be always
long becaufe we pronounce continually *VVe*. *I*, beeing
alone ftanding for the Pronowne *Ego*, in my iudgment
might well be vfed common: but becaufe I neuer fawe
it vfed but fhort I fo obferued it.   Words ending in *y*

I make fhort without doubt, fauing that I haue marked
in others one difference which they vfe in the fame,
that is to make it fhort in the ende ᴜ of an Aduerb, as
gladly, and long in the ende - of an Adiectiue as *goodly*:
but the reafon is as I take it, becaufe the Adiectiue is
or fhould be moft commonly written thus *goodlie.*
O, beeing an Aduerbe is naturally long: in the ende of
wordes both *Monafyllables* and other I thinke it may
be vfed common. The firft of *Pollifyllables* I directed
according to the nature of the worde, as I thought moft
aunfwerable to Latine examples, fauing that fomewhere
I am conftrayned to ftraine curtefy with the prepofition
of a worde compounded or fuch like, which breaketh
no great fquare: as in *defence* or *depart*, etc. The
myddle fillables which are not very many, come for the
moft part vnder the precinct of *Pofition*, whereof fome
of them will not poffibly abide the touch, and therfore
muft needes be a little wrefted: fuch are commonly ye
Aduerbs of three fillables, as *mournfully, fpyghtfully*
and fuch like words, deriued of this Adiectiue, *full*:
and therfore if there be great occafion to vfe them, they
muft be reformed by detracting onely (*l*) and then they
ftand meetely currant, as *mournfuly.* The laft fillables
I wholly directed fo neere as I could to the touch of
common rules.

The moft famous verfe of all the reft, is called *Hexa-
metrum Epicum*, which confifteth of fixe feete, wherof
the firft foure are indifferently either *Spondæi* or *Dactyli*,
the fift is euermore a *dactyl*, aud the fixt a *Spondæ*, as
thus.

$$-\,\cup\,- \quad -\,\cup\,\cup \quad - \quad - \quad -\quad - \quad -\,\cup\,\cup \quad - \quad -$$

Tyterus happily thou liest tumbling vnder a beetchtree.

Thys kinde of verfe I haue onely feene to be practifed
in our Englifh fpeeche: and indeede wyll ftand fomewhat more orderlye therein then any of the other
kindes, vntill we haue fome tolleration of wordes made
by fpeciall rule. The firft that attempted to practife
thys verfe in Englifh, fhould feeme to be the Earle of
Surry, who tranflated fome part of *Virgill* into verfe

indeede, but without regard of true quantity of fillables.
There is one famous *Diftichon*, which is common in the
mouthes of all men, that was made by one Mafter *VVat-
fon*, fellowe of S. *Iohns* Colledge in Cambrydge about
40. yeeres paft, which for the fweetnes and gallantnes
therof in all refpects doth mat[c]h and furpaffe the
Latine coppy of *Horace*, which he made out of *Homers*
wordes, *qui mores hominum etc.*

— ‿ ‿ — — — ‿ ‿ — — — — ‿ ‿——

All trauellers doo gladlie report great praife to Uliffes

— ‿ ‿ — ‿ ‿ — — — — ‿ ‿ ——

For that he knewe manie mens maners, and fa vv many citties.

Which two verfes if they be examined throughout all
the rules and obferuations of the beft verfifying, fhall
bee founde to attaine the very perfection of them all.
There be two other not much inferiour to thefe, which
I found in ye Gloffe of *E. K.* vppon the fift *Æglogue*
of the newe Poet: which Tully tranflated out of Greeke
into Latine, *Hæc habui quæ edi etc.*

All that I eate did I ioy and all that I greedilie gorged.

— — — ‿ ‿ — — — — — ‿ ‿ — —

As for thofe manie goodlie matters left F for others.

Which though they wyll not abide the touch of
Synalæpha in one or two places, yet perhappes fome
Englifh rule which might wyth good reafon be eftablifhed, would make them currant enough, and auoyde
that inconuenience which is very obuious in our
wordes. The great company of famous verfes of thys
fort, which Mafter *Haruey* made, is not vnknowne to
any and are to be viewed at all times. I for my part, fo
farre as thofe examples would leade me, and mine
owne fmall fkyll affoorde me, haue blundered vppon
thefe fewe, whereinto I haue tranflated the two firft
Æglogues of Virgill: becaufe I thought no matter of
mine owne inuention, nor any other of antiquitye
more fitte for tryal of thys thyng, before there were
fome more fpeciall direction, which might leade to a
leffe troublefome manner of wryting.

The Argument of the firft
Æglogue.

Vnder the perfonne of *Tityrus Vyrgill* beeing figured himfelfe, declareth to *Melibeus* an nother Neateheard, the great
benefittes he receyued at *Auguftus* hand, who in the fpoyle
of *Mantua* gaue him hys goods and fubftaunce againe.

𝔐𝔢𝔩𝔦𝔟𝔞𝔢𝔲𝔰.   𝔗𝔦𝔱𝔶𝔯𝔲𝔰.

Tityrus, happilie thou lyste tumbling vnder a beech tree,
  All in a fine oate pipe thefe fweete fongs lustilie chaunting:
VVe, poore foules goe to wracke, and from thefe coastes beremooued,
And fro our pastures fvveete: thou Tityr, at eafe in a shade plott
Makst thicke groues to refound vvith fonges of braue Amarillis.

𝔗𝔦𝔱𝔶𝔯𝔲𝔰.

O Melibæus, *he vvas no man but a God vvho releeude me:*
Euer he shalbe my God: from this fame Sheepcot his alters
Neuer, a tender Lambe fhall vvant, with blood to bedevv them.
This good gift did he giue, to my steeres thus freelie to vvander,
And to my felfe (thou feest) on pipe to refound vvhat J *lifted.*

Melibæus.

Grutch thee fure I doo not, but this thing makes me to vvonder,
VVhence comes all this adoo: vvith grieeuous paine not a little
Can I remooue my Goates: here, Tityre skant get I forvvard
Poore olde crone, tvvo tvvyns at a clappe ith boyfterous hafilles
Left fhe behind, best hope i' my flock laid hard on a bare stone.
Had not a luckleffe lotte poffest our mindes, I remember
VVarnings oft fro the blaft burnt oake vve favv to be fent vs.
Oft did a left hand crovv foretell thefe thinges in her hull tree,
But this God let vs heare what he vvas, good Tityre tell me.

Tityrus.

That fame Cittie fo braue vvhich Rome vvas vvont to be called,
Foole did I thinke, to be like this of ours, vvhere vve to the pastures
VVonted were to remooue from dammes our young prettie Cattell.
Thus did I thinke young vvhelpes, and Kids to be like to the
　　mothers,
Thus did I vvont compare manie great thinges vvith many little.
But this aboue all tovvnes as loftily mounteth her high head,
As by the lovve bafe shrubbes tall Cypreffe shooteth aboue them.

Melibæus.

And vvhat did thee mooue that needes thou must goe to fee Rome?

Tityrus.

Freedome: vvhich though late, yet once lookt backe to my pore
　　ftate,
After time vvhen haires from my beard did ginne to be vvhitish:
Yet lookt back at laft and found me out after a long time.
VVhen Amarill vvas once obtainde, Galatea departed:
For (for I vvill confeffe) vvhilst as Galatea did hold mee,
Hope did I not for freedome, and care had I none to my cattell.
Though manie faire young beastes our folde for the aulters aforded

And manie cheeſes good fro my preſſe vvere ſent to the Cittie:
Seldome times did I bring anie store of pence fro the markett.

Melibaeus.

O Amarill, vvherefore, to thy Gods (very much did I meruaile)
Heauilie thou didſt praie: ripe fruites vngathered all still:
Tityrus is not at home: theſe Pyne trees Tityre miſt thee.
Fountaines longd for thee: theſe hedgrovves vvisht thy return
home

Tityrus.

VVhat vvas then to be doone? from bondage could not Ƒ vvind out:
Neither I could haue found ſuch gentle Gods any vvhere els.
There did I ſee (Melibœe) that youth vvhoſe hestes I by courſe
still.
Fortnights whole to obſerue on the Alters ſure will I not faile.
Thus did he gentlie graunt to my ſute when first I demaunded.
Keepe your heardes poore ſlaues as erst, let bulles to the makes
still.

Melibaeus.

Happy olde man, then thou ſhalt haue thy farme to remaine still,
Large and large to thy ſelfe, others nought but stonie grauell:
And foule ſlymie rush wherewith their lees be beſprinkled.
Here no vnwoonted foode ſhall grieue young theaues who be
laded,
Nor the infections foule of neighbours flocke ſhall annoie them.
Happie olde man. In ſhaddowy bankes and coole prettie places,
Heere by the quainted floodes and ſprings most holie remaining.
Here, theſe quickſets freſh which lands ſeuer out fro thy
neighbors
And greene willow rowes which Hiblœ bees doo reioice in,
Oft fine whistring noiſe, ſhall bring ſweete ſleepe to thy ſences.
Vnder a Rock ſide here will proyner chaunt merrie ditties.
Neither on highe Elme trees, thy beloude Doues loftilie ſitting,
Nor prettie Turtles trim, vvill ceaſe to crooke with a good cheere.

Titprus.

First, therefore fwift buckes shall flie for foode to the skies ward,
And from fish with drawn broade feas themfelues shal auoia
   hence:
First, (both borders broke) Araris fhal run to the Parthanes,
And likewife Tygris shall againe runne backe to the Germanes:
Ere his countnaunce fweete shall flippe once out from my hartroote.

Melibaeus.

VVe poore foules, muft fome to the land cald Affrica packe hence.
Some to the farre Scythia, and fome must to the fwift flood Oaxis.
Some to Britannia coaftes quite parted farre fro the whole world.
Oh thefe paftures pure shall I nere more chance to behold yee?
And our cottage poore with warme turues couerd about trim.
Oh thefe trim tilde landes, fhall a rechleffe fouldier haue them?
And fhall a Barbarian haue this croppe? fee what a mifchiefe
Difcord vile hath araifde? for whom was our labour all tooke?
Novv Melibœe ingraft pœarie stocks, fette vines in an order.
Now goe (my braue flocke once that were) O now goe my
   kidlings.
Neuer againe fhall I now in a greene bowre fweetelie repofed
See ye in queachie briers farre a loofe clambring on a high hill.
Now fhall I fing no Iygges, nor whilst I doo fall to my iunkets.
Shall ye my Goates, cropping fweete flowres and leaues fit
   about me.

Titprus.

Yet thou maist tarrie heere, and keepe me companie this night,
All on a leauie couch: good Aples ripe I doo not lacke,
Chestnutts fweete good store, and plentie of curddes will I fet thee.
Marke i' the Towne how chimnie tops doo beginne to be fmoaking
And fro the Mountaines high how fhaddowes grow to be larger.

The feconde Æglogue called
Alexis.

The Argument.

Virgill in the perfonne of *Corydon* as fome thinke, com-
playneth that he is not fo gratious with Auguftus as he
would bee : or els it is to be referred to a youth *Alexander,*
which was giuen him of *Afinius Pollio,* whom he blameth
for the vnftedfaftnes of his witt and wandering appetite, in
refufing the freendly counfayle which he vfed to giue him.

THat Sheepheard Corydon did burne in loue with Alexis,
   All his mafters deare : and nought had he whereby to hope
Onely in beechen groues, and dolefome fhaddowy places. [for.
Dailie reforted he : there thefe rude difordered outcryes,
Hylles and defert woodes throughout thus mournfully tuned.
O hard harted Alex, haft thou no regard to my fweete fong?
Pyttieft me not a whitt : yea makft me now that I fhall dye.
Yet doo the beaftes find out fine fhades and trim pretty
   coole plottes,
And fro the fun beames fafe lie lyzardes vnder a bufhtufte :·
And for workmen toughe with boyling heate fo beparched,
Garlick fauery fweete and coole hearbes plenty be dreffed.
But, by the fcorcht banke fydes i' thy foote fteppes ftil I goe
   plodding.

Hedgeroweshott doo refound with Grafhops mournfully fqueak-
O had I not ben better abyd Amarillis her anger?   [ing,
And her proude difdaine? yea better abyde my Menalcas?
What though brown did he feeme? yea what though thou be
   fo gallant
O thou fine chery cheekt child truft not t' much to thy beauty.
Black violetts are tooke when dayfes white be refufed.
Me thou doft defpife vnknowne to thy felfe yet Alexis:
What be my riches greate in neate, in milke what aboundance.
In Sicill hylles be my Lambes of which there wander a thoufand.
All times, colde and hote yet frefh milke neuer I wanted.
Such be my Muficke notes, as (when his flockes he recalling)
Amphion of Dirce did vfe on fhore Aracynthus.
Much mifhapt I am not, for late in a bancke I behelde me,
VVhen ftill feas were calme, to thy Daphnis neede not I giue
   place
No, though thou be the iudge, if pictures haue any credite.
O were thou content to remaine with me by the downes heere,
In thefe lodgings fmall, and helpe me proppes to put vnder,
And trym kydling flocke with me to driue to the greene fieldes:
Pan in finging fweete with me fhouldft brauely refemble:
Pan, was firft the inuenter, pypes to adioyne in an order:
Pan, poore flockes and Sheepheardes to moft duly regardeth.
Thofe fine lips thou needft not feare to brufe with a fweete pype:
VVhat dyd Amynt forfake i'this excercife to be cunning?
One pype with feauene fundry ftops matcht fweetly together.
Haue I my felfe, Damætas which ats death he bequeathd me,
And fayd, heere, thou art now the fecond which euer hath ought
So fayd Damætas: but Amyntas fpightfully fcornde it.   [it.
Alfo, two pretty fmall wyld kyddes, moft goodlie befpotted
Haue I, that heere i' the dales doo runne skant fafe I doo
   feare me.
Twyce in a day two teates they fuck: for thee will I keepe them:
Wondrous faine to haue had them both was Theftylis of late.
And fo fhe fhall: for I fee thou fcornft whatfo-euer I giue thee.
Come hyther O thou fweete face boy: fee fee, to thy felfe heere
How fayre Nymphes in baskets full doo bring manie Lillies:
White violets fweete Nais plucks and bloomes fro the Poppies,
Narcyfs, and dyll flowres moft fweete that fauoureth alfo.

Cafia, broade mary Goldes, with pancyes, and Hyacinthus.
And I my felfe rype peaches foft as filke will I gather.
And fuch Chefnutts as Amarill was wont to reioyce at.
Ploms wyll I bring likewife: that fruite fhall be honored alfo.
And ye O Lawrell twygges that I croppe, and myrte thy
felfe next.
For ye be wont, (bound both in a bunch) moft fweetely to
fauour.
Thou art but a Clowne Corydon: thefe gifts efteemes not Alexis:
Nor by thy gifts to obtaine art meete to incounter Iolas.
VVretch (ahlas) whats this that I wifh? fouth blafts to the
yong flowers
Or cleere cryftall ftreames with loathfome fwyne to be troubled.
Ah mad boy from whom dooft runne? why Gods ithe woods
dwelt:
And Paris erft of Troy: Pallas moft gladly reioyfeth,
In thefe bowres: and in trym groues we all chiefely delight
vs.
Grym Lyoneffe doth courfe curft woolues, fo wolues doo
the kydlinges.
And thefe wanton Kyddes likewife thefe faire Cytifus
flowers.
Thee Corydon (O Alex) fome pleafure euery wight pulles.
See thefe yoked fteeres fro the plough nowe feeme to be
lett loofe.
And thefe fhadowes large doo declare thys fun to depart
hence
Styll I doo burne in loue. What meane in loue to be lookt
for?
Ah Corydon Corydon, what raging fury dooth haunt thee,
Halfe cropt downe be thy vynes and broade brauncht elmes
ouerhang them.
Rather about fome needefull worke now bufy thy felfe well,
Either on Ofyers tuffe or bulrufh weaue pretty basketts.
And if Alexis fcorne thee ftill, mayft hope for another.

FINIS.

I durſt not enterpryſe to goe any further with this rude tranſlation: beeing for the reſpects aforeſayd a troubleſome and vnpleaſant peece of labour: And therefore theſe ſhall ſuffice till further occaſion ſhall ſerue to imploy ſome profitable paynes in this behalfe.

The next verſe in dignity to the *Hexameters*, is ye *Carmen Elegiacum* which confiſteth of foure feete and two od ſillables: viz: the two firſt feete, eyther *Dactyli* or *Spondæi* indifferent, the one long ſillable: next two *Dactyli* and an other long ſillable − − − ∪ ∪ − − ∪ ∪ − ∪ ∪ − ſome doo meaſure it in this forte (and more truely yet not ſo readily to all) accounting firſt two indifferently either *Dactyli* or *Spondæi*, then one *Spondæi*, and two *Anapæſti*. But it commeth all to one reckoning. Thys verſe is alwayes vnſeperably adioyned vnto the Hexameter, and ſerueth eſpecially to the handling of loue and dalliances, whereof it taketh the name. It will not frame altogether ſo currantlye in our Engliſh as the other, becauſe the ſhortneſſe of the feconde *Penthimimer* will hardly be framed to fall together in good ſence, after the Latine rules. I haue not ſeene very many of them made by any, and therefore one or two for example ſake ſhall be ſufficient.

This *Diſtichon* out of *Ouid*.

> *Ingenium quondam fuerat pretioſius auro,*
> *At nunc barbaries grandis habere nihil.*

May thus be tranſlated.

Learning once was thought to be better then any gold was,
Now he that hath not wealth is but a barbarian.

> And thys
>
> *Omnia funt hominum tenui pendentia filo:*
> *Et ſubito caſu quæ valuere ruunt.*

Tis but a ſlender thread, which all mens ſtates do depend on:
And moſt goodly thinges quickly doo fall to decay.

As for the verfes *Phalocium* and *Iambicum*, I haue
not as yet made any tryall in them: but the *Sapphic* I
affure you, in my iudgment wyl doo very pretty, if ye
wants which I fpeake were once fupplied. For tryall
of which I haue turned the new Poets fweete fong of
Eliza into fuch homely *Sapphick* as I coulde.

Thys verfe confifteth of thefe fiue feete, one *Chore*,
one *fpondæ*, one *dactyl*, and two *Choreis*, with this
addition, that after euery third verfe be fette one
Adonium verfe, which confifteth of a *dactyl* and a
fpondæ. It is more troublefome and tedious to frame
in our fpeeche by reafon they runne without difference,
euery verfe being a like in quantity throughout, yet in
my iudgement ftandeth meetely well in the fame. I
pray looke the Coppy which I haue tranflated in the
fourth *Æglogue* of the *Sheepheardes Calender*: ye fong
of *Colins* making which *Hobbinoll* fingeth in prayfe
of the Queenes maiefty, vnder the name of *Eliza*.

YE dainty Nymphes that in this bleffed brooke,
   doo bathe your breft:
Forfake your watry bowres and hether looke,
   at my requeft:
And onely you Virgins that on *Parnafs* dwell.
Whence floweth *Helicon* the learned well,
   helpe me to blafe
   her worthy praife
That in her fex doth all excell.

Of fayre *Eliza* be your filuer fong
   that bleffed wight:
The flowre of Virgins, may fhe flourifh long,
   in princely plight.
For fhe is *Syrinx* daughter without fpott,
Which *Pan* the Sheepheards God on her begot:
   fo fprang her grace,
   of heauenly race,
No mortall blemifh may her blott.

See where fhe fittes, etc.

F

The *Saphick* verfe.

```
— ᴜ — — — ᴜ ᴜ — ᴜ — —
— ᴜ — — — ᴜ ᴜ — ᴜ — —
— ᴜ — — — ᴜ ᴜ — ᴜ — —
        — ᴜ ᴜ — —
```

O ye Nymphes moft fine who refort to this brooke,
For to bathe there your pretty breafts at all times :
Leaue the watrifh bowres, hyther and to me come
                   at my requeft nowe.

And ye Virgins trymme who refort to *Parnafs*,
Whence the learned well *Helicon* beginneth :
Helpe to blafe her worthy deferts, that all els
                   mounteth aboue farre.

Nowe the filuer fonges of *Eliza* fing yee,
Princely wight whofe peere not among the virgins
Can be found : that long fhe may remaine among vs.
                   now let vs all pray.

For *Syrinx* daughter fhe is, of her begotten
Of the great God *Pan*, thus of heauen aryfeth,
All her exlent race : any mortall harde happe
                   cannot aproche her.

See, fhe fittes moft feemely in a graffy greene plott,
Clothed in weedes meete for a princely mayden,
Bofte with Ermines white, in a goodly fcarlett
                   brauely befeeming.

Decked is that crowne that vpon her head ftandes
With the red Rofe and many Daffadillies,
Bayes, the Primrofe and violetts, be fette by : how
                   ioyfull a. fight ift.

Say, behold did ye euer her Angelike face,
Like to *Phœbe* fayre ? or her heauenly hauour
And the princelike grace that in her remaineth ?
                   haue yee the like feene ?

Medled ift red rofe with a white together
Which in either cheeke do depeinct a trymme cheere,
Her maieftie and eye to behold fo comely, her
                   like who remembreth ?

Phœbus once peept foorth with a goodly guilt hewe,
For to gaze : but when he fawe the bright beames
Spread abroade fro' her face with a glorious grace,
                                                it did amaze him.

When another funne he behelde belowe heere,
Blufht he red for fhame, nor againe he durfl looke:
Would he durfl bright beames of his owne with hers match,
                                                for to be vanquifht.

Shew thy felfe now *Cynthia* with thy cleere rayes,
And behold her: neuer abafht be thou fo: [beauty, how
When fhe fpreades thofe beames of her heauenly
                                                thou art in a dump dafht?

But I will take heede that I match not her grace, .
With the *Laton* feede, *Niobe* that once did,
Nowe fhe doth therefore in a ftone repent: to all
                                                other a warning.

Pan he may well boafte that he did begit her
Such a noble wight, to *Syrinx* is it ioy,
That fhe found fuch lott with a bellibone trym
                                                for to be loaden.

When my younglinges firfl to the dammes doo bleat out,
Shall a milke white Lambe to my Lady be offred : [grome.
For my Goddeffe fhee is yea I my felfe her Heard-
                                                though but a rude Clowne.

Vnto that place *Caliope* dooth high her,
Where my Goddeffe fhines: to the fame the Mufer
After her with fweete Violines about them
                                                cheerefully tracing

Is not it Bay braunche that aloft in handes they haue,
Eune to giue them fure to my Lady *Eliza* :
O fo fweete they play—and to the fame doo fing too
                                                heaunly to heare ifl.

See, the Graces trym to the ftroake doo foote it,
Deftly dauncing, and meriment doo make them,
Sing to the inftruments to reioyce the more, but
                                                wants not a fourth grace?

Then the daunce wyll be eune, to my Lady therefore
Shalbe geune that place, for a grace fhe fhall be
For to fill that place that among them in heaune, fhe
　　　　　　　　　　　may be receiued.

Thys beuy of bright Nymphes, whether ift goe they now?
Raunged all thus fine in a rowe together?
They be Ladies all i' the Lake behight foe?
　　　　　　　　　　　they thether all goe.

One that is there chiefe that among the reft goes,
Called is *Chores* of Olyues fhe beares a
Goodly Crownett, meete for a Prince that in peace
　　　　　　　　　　　euer abideth.

All ye Sheepheardes maides that about the greene dwell,
Speede ye there to her grace, but among ye take heede
All be Virgins pure that aproche to deck her,
　　　　　　　　　　　duetie requireth.

When ye fhall prefent ye before her in place,
See ye not your felues doo demeane too rudely:
Bynd the fillets: and to be fine the wafte gyrt
　　　　　　　　　　　faft with a tawdryne

Bring the Pinckes therewith many Gelliflowres fweete,
And the Cullambynes: let vs haue the Wynefops,
With the Cornation that among the loue laddes
　　　　　　　　　　　wontes to be worne much.

Daffadowndillies all a long the ground ftrowe,
And the Cowflyppe with a pretty paunce let heere lye.
Kyngcuppe and Lillies fo beloude of all men
　　　　　　　　　　　And the deluce flowre.

　One verfe there remaineth vntranflated as yet, with
fome other of this forte, which I meant to haue finifhed,
but by reafon of fome let which I had, I am con-
ftrained to defer to fome other time, when I hope to
gratify the Readers with more and better verfes of this
fort: for in trueth I am perfwaded a little paine taking
might furnifh our fpeeche with as much pleafaunt
delight in this kinde of verfe, as any other whatfoeuer.

Heere followe the Cannons or generall cautions of Poetry, prefcribed by Horace,
firft gathered by *Georgius Fabricius Cremni-*
cenfis: which I thought good to annex to
thys Treatife, as very neceffary obferuations
to be marked of all Poets.

In his Epiftle ad Pifones
de arte Poetica.

Irft let the inuention be meete for the
matter, not differing, or ftraunge,
or monftrous. For a womans head,
a horfe necke, the bodie of a
dyuers coloured Byrd, and many
members of fundry creatures com-
pact together, whofe legges ending
like a Fyfhes tayle: this in a picture
is a wonderful deformitie: but if there be fuch
diuerfitye in the frame of a fpeeche, what can be
more vncomely or ilfauoured?

2. The ornaments or colours muft not bee too many,
nor rafhly aduentured on, neither muft they be vfed
euery where and thruft into euery place.

3. The proprietie of fpeeche muft bee duely obferued
that wayghty and great matters be not fpoken flenderly,
or matters of length too briefly: for it belongeth much
both to the comlineffe and nature of a matter: that

in big matters there be lykewife vfed boyfterous wordes.

4. In Poeticall defcriptions, the fpeeche muft not exceede all credite, nor any thing fainedlie brought in, againft all courfe of nature.

5. The difpofing of the worke muft be fuch, that there be no offence committed, as it were by too ex-quifite dilligence: for many thinges may be oft com-mitted, and fome thing by too curious handling be made offenciue. Neyther is it in one part to be well furnifhed, and in another to be neglected. Which is prooued by example of a Caruer, who expreffed very artificially the heade and vpper part of a body, but the reft hee could not make an ende of. Againe, it is prooued thus, that a body fhould not be in other partes beautifull, and yet bee deformed in the crooked nofe: for all the members in a well fhapen bodie muft be aunfwerable, found, and well proportioned.

6. He that taketh in hande to write any thing muft firft take heede that he be fufficient for the fame: for often vnwary fooles through their rafhnes are ouertooke with great want of ability

7. The ornament of a worke confifteth in wordes, and in the manner of the wordes, are either fimple or mixt, newe or olde, propper or tranflated. In them all good iudgment muft be vfed and ready wytt. The chiefeft grace is in the moft frequented wordes, for the fame reafon holdeth in wordes, as doth in coynes, that the moft vfed and tried are beft efteemed.

8. The kinde of verfe is to be confidered and aptly applied to the argument, in what meafure is moft meete for euery fort. The moft vfuall kindes are foure, the *Heroic, Elegiac, Iambick,* and *Lyric.*

9. One muft vfe one kynde of fpeeche alike in all wrytings. Sometime the *Lyric* ryfeth aloft, fometime the comicall. To the Tragicall wryters belong properly the bygge and boyfterous wordes. Examples muft be interplaced according fitly to the time and place.

10. Regarde is to be had of affections: one thing

becommeth pleaſant perſons, an other ſadde, an other
wrathfull, an other gentle, which muſt all be heedefully
reſpected, Three thinges therefore are requiſite in
verſes, beauty, ſweetnes, and the affection. *Theo-
phraſtus* ſayth that this beauty or delectableneſſe is a
deceyt, and Ariſtotle calleth it τυραννία ὀλιγοκρονίον, a
momentany tyrany. Sweetneſſe retayneth a Reader,
affection moueth him.

11. Euery perſon muſt be fitted accordingly, and the
ſpeeche well ordered: wherein are to be conſidered the
dignity, age, ſex, fortune, condition, place, Country, etc.
of eche perſon.

12. The perſonnes are eyther to be ſayned by the
Poets them ſelues, or borrowed of others, if he borrow
them, then muſt hee obſerue το ὅμοιον, that is, that
he folow that Author exactly whom he purpoſeth to
immitate, and whereout he bringeth his examples.
But if he ſayne newe perſonnes, then muſt he keepe
his το ὁμαλόν, that is equallie: ſo bringing them in eche
place, that it be alwayes agreeable, and the laſt like
vnto the firſt, and not make one perſon nowe a bolde
boaſter, and the ſame ſtraightwaies a wiſe warie man,
for that is paſſing abſurd. Againe, euery one muſt
obſerue το ἅρμοστον, which is interpreted *conuenientiam*,
fitneſſe: as it is meete and agreeable euery where, a
man to be ſtoute, a woman fearefull, a ſeruant crafty,
a young man gentle.

13. Matters which are common may be handled by a
Poet as they may be thought propper to himſelfe alone.
All matters of themſelues are open to be intreated of
by any man: but if a thing be handled of ſome one in
ſuch ſort, as he thereby obtaine great prayſe, he maketh
it his owne or propper to himſelfe, as many did write
of the Troiane war, but yet *Homer* made matter which
was common to all, propper to himſelfe.

14. Where many thinges are to be taken out of
auncienter tongues, as the Latines tooke much out of
the Greekes, the wordes are not ſo preciſelie to be followed, but that they bee altered according to the iudg-

ment and will of the Immitator, which precept is borrowed of Tully, *Non verbum verbo necefse est reddere.*

15. The beginning muft not be foolifhly handled,
that is, ftraungly or too long.

16. The propofition or narration let it not be far
fetched or vnlikely, and in the fame forget not the differences of ages and perfons.

17. In a Comedie it is needfull to exhibite all the
actions openlie, as fuch as are cruell, vnhoneft, or ougly,
but fuch thinges may better bee declared by fome meete
and handfome wordes, after what forte they are fuppofed to bee doone.

18. If a Commedye haue more Actes then fiue, it is
tedious, if fewer, it is not fufficient.

It fytteth not to bring in the perfonnes of Gods, but
in verie great matters. *Cicero* fayth, when the Tragedy wryters cannot bring theyr matters to good paffe,
they runne to God. Let not more perfonnes fpeake
together then foure for auoyding confufion.

The *Chori* muft be well garnifhed and fette foorth :
wherein eyther menne are admonifhed, or reprehended,
or counfayled vnto vertue. Such matter muft bee
chofen for the *Chorus*, as may bee meete and agreeable
to that which is in hand. As for inftruments and finging, they are Reliques of olde fimplicitye. For the
Muficke commonlye vfed at Theaters and the licen-
cioufneffe of theyr fonges, which together wyth theyr
wealth increafed among the Romaines, is hurtfull to
difcipline and good manners.

19. In a *Satyr* the clownifh company and rurall Gods,
are brought in to temperate the Heauineffe of Tragedies, wyth fome myrth and paftyme. In iefting it muft
be obferued that it bee not lacyuious or Rybaldlike, or
flaunderous, which precept holdeth generallie in all
fortes of wrytynges.

In a *Satyr* greate heede is to be taken, of the place,
of the day, and of the perfonnes : as of *Bacchus, Silenus,*
or the *Satyres.* Againe of the vnmeetneffe or inconuenience of the matter, and of the wordes that they be

fitted according to the perſons: of *Decorum*, that he
which repreſented ſome noble perſonage in the Tragedie, bee not ſome buſy foole in the *Satyr*: finallie of
the hearers, leaſt they bee offended by myxing filthy
matters with ieſtes, wanton toyes wyth vnhoneſt, or
noyſome with merry thinges.

20. The feete are to be applied propper to euery
kinde of verſe, and therin a Poet muſt not vſe too
much licence or boldnes. The auncient writers in
Iambick verſes vſed at firſt pure *Iambicks*: Afterwards
Spondæus was admitted into *Locos impares*, but at laſt
ſuch was the licentious cuſtome, that they woulde
both *Spondæus* where they liſted, and other feete
without regarde.

21. In compyling of verſes great care and circum-
ſpection muſt be vſed.

Thoſe verſes which be made Extempore, are of no
great eſtimation: thoſe which are vnartificiall, are
vtterly repelled as too fooliſh. Though many doo
lightlie regard our verſes, yet ought the Carelefneſſe of
the hearers to bee no cauſe in vs of errour and negligence. Who defireth to make any thing worthy to be
heard of learned eares, let hym reade Greeke Authors
heedefullie and continually.

22. Artes haue their increaſinges euen as other
things, beeing naturall, ſo haue Tragedies which were
firſt rudely inuented by *Theſpis*, at laſt were much
adorned by *Æſchylus*: at the firſt they were practiſed
in Villages of the Countrey, afterwardes brought to
ſtages in great Citties.

23. Some Artes doo increaſe, ſome doo decay by a
certayne naturall courſe. The olde manner of Commedies decayde, by reaſon of ſlaundering which therein
they vſed againſt many, for which there was a penaltie
appointed, leaſt their bitternes ſhould proceede too
farre: In place of which among the Latines came the
Satyres.

The auncient Authors of Comedies, were *Eupolis*,
Cratinus, and *Ariſtophanes*, of the middle ſorte *Plato*

Comicus, of the laft kinde *Menander*, which continued and was accounted the moft famous.

24. A Poet fh ould not content himfelfe onely with others inuentions, but himfelfe alfo by ye example of old wryters fholde bring fomething of his owne induftry, which may bee laudable. So did they which writte among the Latines the Comedies called *Togatæ*, whofe arguments were taken from ye Greekes, and the other which wrytt the *Pretextatæ*, whereof the arguments were Latine.

25. Heedefulneffe and good compofition maketh a perfecte verfe, and that which is not fo may be reprehended. The faculty of a goode witte exceedeth Arte.

26. A Poet that he may be perfect, hath neede to haue knowledge of that part of Philofophy which informeth ye life to good manners. The other which pertaineth to naturall thinges, is leffe plaufible, hath fewer ornaments, and is not fo profitable.

27. A Poet to the knowledge of Philofophie fhoulde alfo adde greater experience, that he may know the fafhions of men and difpofitions of people. Thys profit is gott by trauelling, that whatfoeuer he wryteth he may fo expreffe and order it, that hys narration may be formable.

28. The ende of Poetry is to wryte pleafant thinges, and profitable. Pleafant it is which delighteth by beeing not too long, or vneafy to be kept in memory, and which is fomewhat likelie, and not altogether forged. Profitable it is, which ftyrreth vppe the mindes to learning and wifedome.

29. Certaine efcapes are to be pardoned in fome Poets, fpecially in great workes. A faulte may bee committed either in refpect of hys propper Arte, or in fome other Arte: that a Poet fhoulde erre in precepts of hys owne arte, is a fhamefull thing, to committe a faulte in another Arte is to be borne withal: as in *Virgil*, who fayneth that *Æneas* comming into *Affrica* flew with hys darte certaine Stagges, whereas

indeede *Affrica* hath in it none of thofe beaftes. Such
errours doo happen eyther by vnheedefulnes, when
one efcapeth them by negligence: or by the common
fragility of man, becaufe none there is which can
know all thinges. Therefore this laft kinde of errour
is not to be ftucke vppon.

30. A good Poet fhould haue refpect to thys, how
to retaine hys Reader or hearer. In a picture fome
thing delighteth beeing fette farre of, fomething nearer,
but a Poet fhould delight in all places as well in funne
as fhaddowe.

31. In a Poet is no meane to be admitted, which if
hee bee not he of all is the worft of all.

32. A Poeme if it runne not fweetely and fmoothly
is odious: which is proued by a *fimile* of the two
fenfes, hearing and tafting, as in fweete and pleafaunt
meates. And the Poem muft bee of that forte, that
for the fweeteneffe of it may bee acceptable and continue like it felfe vnto the ende, leaft it wearye or
driue away a Reader.

33. He that would wryte any thing worthy the pof-
teritye, let him not enterprife any thing wherevnto his
nature is not agreeable. *Mercury* is not made of wood (as
they fay) neyther doth *Minerua* fauour all ftudies in
euery one. In all Artes nature is the beft helpe, and
learned men vfe commonly to fay that *A Poet is as well
borne as made a Poet.*

34. Let no man efteeme himfelfe fo learned, but that
he may fubmytte hys wrytinges to the iudgments of
others, and correct and throughly amend the fame
himfelfe.

35. The profitte of Poetry fprang thus, for that the
auncient wyfe men fet downe the beft things that per-
tained to mans life, manners, or felicity, and examining
and proouing the fame by long experience of time,
when they are aged they publifhed them in wrytinges.
The vfe of Poetry what it was at the firft, is manifeft
by the examples of the mofte learned men: as of
Orpheus who firft builded houfes: of *Amphion* who

made Citties, of *Tyrtæus* who firſt made warre: of
Homer, who wryt moſt wyſely.

36. In an artificiall Poet three thinges are requiſite,
nature, Arte, and dilligence.

37. A wryter muſt learne of the learned, and he
muſt not ſticke to confeſſe when he erreth: that the
worſe he may learne to auoyde, and knowe howe to
follow the better.

The confeſſion of an errour betoken a noble and a
gentle minde. *Celſus* and *Quintillian* doo report of
Hippocrates, that leaſt he ſhould deceiue his poſterity,
he confeſſed certayne errours, as it well became an
excellent minded man, and one of great credite. For
(as ſayth *Celſus*) light witts becauſe they haue nothing,
wyll haue nothing taken from them.

38. In making choiſe of ſuch freendes as ſhould tell
vs the trueth, and correct our wrytinges, heedefull
iudgment muſt bee vſed: leaſt eyther we chooſe vn-
ſkylfull folke, or flatterers, or diſſemblers. The vnſkil-
full know not how to iudge, flatterers feare to offende,
diſſemblers in not prayſing doo ſeeme to commende.

39. Let no man deceiue himſelfe, or ſuffer himſelfe
to be deceiued, but take ſome graue learned man to be
iudge of his dooing, and let him according to hys
counſayle change and put out what hee thinketh good.

40. He which will not flatter and is of ability to
iudge, let him endeuour to nothing ſo much, as to the
correction of that which is wrytten, and that let be
doone with earneſt and exquiſite iudgment. He which
dooth not thus, but offendeth wilfully in breaking his
credite too raſhly, may be counted for a madde, furious,
and franticke foole.

41. The faultes commonly in verſes are ſeauen, as
either they be deſtitute of Arte, of facility, or ornament:
or els, they be ſuperfluous, obſcure, ambicious, or
needeleſſe.

Out of the Epiftles ad Mecænatem, Auguftum, et Florum.

42. An immitation fhould not be too feruile or fuper-flitious, as though one durft not varry one iotte from the example: neyther fhould it be fo fenceleffe or vn-fkilfull, as to immitate thinges which are abfurde, and not to be followed.

43. One fhould not altogether treade in the fteppes of others, but fometime he may enter into fuch wayes as haue not beene haunted or vfed of others. *Horace* borrowed ye *Iambick* verfe of *Archilocus*, expreffing fully his numbers and elegant[l]y, but his vnfeemely wordes and pratling tauntes hee moftewyfhlye fhunned.

44. In our verfes we fhould not gape after the phrafes of the fimpler forte, but ftriue to haue our writings allowable in the iudgments of learned menne.

45. The common peoples iudgments of Poets is feldome true, and therefore not to be fought after. The vulgar fort in *Rome* iudged *Pacuuious* to be very learned, *Accius* to bee a graue wryter, that *Affranius* followed *Menander*, *Plautus*, *Epicharmus*: that *Terence* excelled in Arte *Cæcilius* in grauity: but the learned forte were not of this opinion. There is extant in *Macrobius* (I knowe not whether *Angellius*) the like verdite concerning them which wryt *Epigrammes*. That *Catullus* and *Caluus* wrytt fewe thinges that were good, *Næuius* obfcure, *Hortenfius* vncomely, *Cynna* vnpleafant, and *Memmius* rough.

46. The olde wryters are fo farre to be commended, as nothing be taken from the newe: neyther may we thinke but that the way lyeth open ftyll to others to

attaine to as great matters. Full well fayd *Sido.ùus* to
Eucherius, I reuerence the olde wryters, yet not fo as
though I leffe efteemed the vertues and defertes of the
wryters in this age.

47. Newnes is gratefull if it be learned: for certaine
it is, Artes are not bothe begunne and perfected at
once, but are increafed by time and ftudie. which
notwithftanding when they are at the full perfection,
doo debate and decreafe againe.

Cic. de orat. There is nothing in the world which
burfteth out all at once, and commeth to light all
wholly together.

48. No man fhould dare to practife an Arte that is
daungerous, efpecially before he haue learned the
fame perfectly: fo doo guyders of Shyppes: fo doo
Phifitions: but fo did not manie Romaine Poets (yea
fo doo not too many Englifh wryters) who in a certaine
corragious heate gaped after glory by wryting verfes,
but fewe of them obtayned it.

49. A Poet fhould be no leffe fkylfull in dealing
with the affectes of the mynde, then a tumbler or a
Iuggler fhoulde bee ready in his Arte. And with fuch
pyth fhoulde he fette foorth hys matters, that a Reader
fhoulde feeme not onely to heare the thing, but to fee
and be prefent at the dooing thereof. Which faculty
Fabius calleth ὑποτασιν and *Ariftotle* προ ομματον θεσιν
ἡ ποίησιμ.

50. Poets are either fuch as defire to be liked of on
ftages, as Commedie and Tragedie wryters: or fuch as
woulde bee regeftred in Libraries. Thofe on ftages
haue fpeciall refpect to the motions of the minde, that
they may ftirre bothe the eyes and eares of their
beholders. But the other which feeke to pleafe
priuately with[in] the walles, take good aduifement in
their workes, that they may fatiffy the exact iudgments
of learned men in their ftudies.

51. A Poet fhoulde not bee too importunate, as to
offende in vnfeafonable fpeeches: or vngentle, as to
contemne the admonitions of others: or ambicious, as

to thinke too well of his owne dooinges: or too way-
ward, as to thinke, reward enough cannot be gyuen him
for his deferte, or finally too proude, as to defyre to
be honoured aboue meafure.

52. The emendations of Poemes be very neceffary,
that in the obfcure poyntes many thinges may be
enlightned, in the bafer partes many thinges may be
throughly garnifhed. Hee may take away and put
out all vnpropper and vnfeemely words, he may with
difcretion immitate the auncient wryters, he may
abridge thinges that are too lofty, mittigate thynges
that are too rough, and may vfe all remedies of fpeeche
throughout the whole worke. The thinges which are
fcarce feemely, he may amende by Arte and methode.

53. Let a Poet firft take vppon him, as though he
were to play but an Actors part, as he may bee
efteemed like one which wryteth without regarde,
neyther let him fo pollifh his works, but that euery
one for the bafeneffe thereof, may think to make as
good. Hee may likewyfe exercife the part of gefturer,
as though he feemed to meddle in rude and common
matters, and yet not fo deale in them, as it were for
variety fake, nor as though he had laboured them
thoroughly but tryfled with them, nor as though he
had fweat for them, but practifed a little. For fo to
hyde ones cunning, that nothing fhould feeme to bee
laborfome or exquifite, when notwithftanding, euery
part is pollifhed with care and ftudie, is a fpeciall gyft
which *Ariftotle* calleth κρῆψν.

54. It is onely a poynt of wyfedome, to vfe many
and choyfe elegant words, but to vnderftand alfo and
to fet foorth thinges which pertaine to the happy ende
of mans life. Wherevppon the Poet *Horace*, calleth
the Arte poeticall, without the knowledge of learning
and philofophy, a *prating vanity*. Therfore a good
and allowable Poet, muft be adorned with wordes,
plentious in fentences, and if not equall to an Orator,
yet very neere him, and a fpecial louer of learned men.

F I N I S.

Epilogus.

His fmall trauell (courteous Reader) I defire thee take in good worth: which I haue compyled, not as an exquifite cenfure concerning this matter, but (as thou mayft well perceiue, and) in trueth to that onely ende that it might be an occafion, to haue the fame throughly and with greater difcretion, taken in hande and laboured by fome other of greater abilitie : of whom I knowe there be manie among the famous Poets in London, who bothe for learning and leyfure, may handle this Argument far more pythilie then my felfe. Which if any of them wyll vouchfafe to doo, I truft wee fhall haue Englifhe Poetry at a higher price in fhort fpace : and the rabble of balde Rymes fhall be turned to famous workes, comparable (I fuppofe) with the beft workes of Poetry in other tongues. In the meane time, if my poore fkill, can fette the fame any thing forwarde, I wyll not ceafe to practife the fame towardes the framing of fome apt Englifh *Profodia:* ftyll hoping, and hartelie wifhing to enioy firft the benefitte of fome others iudgment, whofe authority may beare greater credite, and whofe learning can better performe it.

(∴)

Turnbull & Spears, Printers, Edinburgh.

A List of WORKS

Edited by

Professor EDWARD ARBER

F.S.A. ; Fellow of King's College, London ; Hon. Member of the Virginia and Wisconsin Historical Societies; late English Examiner at the London University; and also at the Victoria University, Manchester; Emeritus Professor of English Language and Literature, Mason College, Birmingham.

An English Garner

English Reprints

The War Library

The English Scholar's Library

The first Three English Books on America

The first English New Testament, 1526

The Paston Letters, 1422–1509.   Edited by JAMES GAIRDNER.   3 vols.

A List of 837 London Publishers, 1553–1640

All the Works in this Catalogue are published at net prices.

ARCHIBALD CONSTABLE AND CO.,

14, PARLIAMENT ST., WESTMINSTER.

NOTE

THE ENGLISH GARNER, THE ENGLISH REPRINTS, *and* THE ENGLISH SCHOLAR'S LIBRARY *are now issued in a new style of binding. A few copies in the old style are still to be had, and will be supplied if specially ordered, as long as the stock lasts. Some of Professor Arber's Publications can still be supplied on Large Paper. Prices on application to the Booksellers or from the Publishers.*

ARCHIBALD CONSTABLE & CO.

An English Garner

INGATHERINGS FROM OUR HISTORY AND LITERATURE.

₊ *Abridged Lists of the Texts ; many of which are very rare, and not obtainable in any other form.*

VOL I.

Large Crown 8vo, cloth, 5s. net.

English Political, Naval, and Military History, etc., etc.

English Voyages, Travels, Commerce, etc., etc.

English Life and Progress.

English Literature, Literary History, and Biography.

English Poetry.

VOL II.

Large Crown 8vo, cloth, 5s. net.

English Political, Naval, and Military History, etc., etc.

1. The Triumph at Calais and Boulogne of HENRY VIII. [with ANNE BOLEYN] and FRANCIS I.   November, 1532.
2. The Coronation Procession of Queen ANNE [BOLEYN] from the Tower through London to Westminster.   June, 1533.
3. English Army Rations in 1591.
4. Rev. T. PRINCE. A History of New England in the form of Annals, from 1602 to 1633.   Published at Boston, N.E., in 1736-1755.   This is the most exact condensed account in existence of the foundation of our first Colonies in America.

English Voyages, Travels, Commerce, etc., etc.

5. Captain T. SANDERS. The unfortunate voyage of the *Jesus* to Tripoli, where the crew were made slaves.   1584-1585.
6. N. H. The Third Circumnavigation of the Globe, by THOMAS CAVENDISH, in the *Desire*.   1586-1588.
7. The famous fight of the *Dolphin* against Five Turkish Men-of-War off Cagliari.   1617.

English Life and Progress.

8. Dr. J. DEE. The Petty Navy Royal. [Fisheries].   1577.
9. Captain HITCHCOCK. A Political Plat [*Scheme*], etc. [Herring Fisheries.]
10. D. DEFOE. The Education of Women.   1692.

English Literature, Literary History, and Biography.

11. F. MERES. A Sketch of English Literature, etc., up to September, 1598.   This is the most important contemporary account of SHAKESPEARE'S Works to this date ; including some that have apparently perished.
12. J. WRIGHT. The Second Generation of English Actors, 1625-1670.   This includes some valuable information respecting London Theatres during this period.

English Poetry.

13. Sir P. SIDNEY. Sonnets and Poetical Translations.   Before 1587.
14. H. CONSTABLE, *and others*.   DIANA.   [Sonnet.]   1594.
15. Madrigals, Elegies, and Poems, by various other Poets.

VOL. III.

Large Crown 8vo, cloth, 5s. net.

English Political, Naval, and Military History, etc., etc.

1. W. PATTEN. The Expedition into Scotland : with the Battle of Pinkie Cleugh or Musselburgh, 1547. This was the " Rough Wooing of MARY, Queen of Scots," whom the English wanted to marry EDWARD VI.

English Voyages, Travels, Commerce, etc., etc.

2. J. H. VAN LINSCHOTEN. Voyage to Goa and back, in Portuguese carracks. 1583-1592.
This work showed the way to the East, and led to the formation of the Dutch and the English East India Companies. For nearly three years this Dutchman, returning in charge of a cargo of pepper, spices, etc., was pinned up in the Azores by the English ships ; of whose daring deeds he gives an account.
3. E. WRIGHT. The voyage of the Earl of CUMBERLAND to the Azores in 1589. This is a part of LINSCHOTEN'S story re-told more fully from an English point of view.
4. The first Englishmen—JOHN NEWBERY and RALPH FITCH —that ever reached India overland, *viâ* Aleppo and the Persian Gulf, in 1583-1589. They met with LINSCHOTEN there ; and also T. Stevens, the Jesuit, see vol. i. p. 130.

English Life and Progress.

5. J. CAIUS, M.D. Of English Dogs. 1536. Translated from the Latin by A. FLEMING in 1576.
6. Britain's Buss. A Computation of the Cost and Profit of a Herring Buss or Ship. 1615.

English Literature, Literary History, and Biography.

7. T. ELLWOOD. Relations with J. MILTON. This young Quaker rendered many services to the Poet ; amongst which was the suggestion of *Paradise Regained.*
8. J. DRYDEN. Of Dramatic Poesy. An Essay. This charming piece of English Prose was written in 1665 and published in 1668. With it is given the entire Controversy between DRYDEN and Sir R. HOWARD on this subject.

English Poetry.

9. S. DANIEL. DELIA. [Sonnets.] 1594.
10. T. CAMPION, M.D. Songs and Poems. 1601-1613.
11. Lyrics, Elegies, etc., by other Poets.

VOL IV.

Large Crown 8vo, cloth, 5s. net.

English Political, Naval, and Military History, etc., etc.

1. E. UNDERHILL, "the Hot Gospeller," Imprisonment in 1553, with Anecdotes of Queen MARY's Coronation Procession, WYATT's Rebellion, the Marriage of PHILIP and MARY, etc.

2. J. FOX. The Imprisonment of the Princess ELIZABETH. 1554–1555.

3. Texts relating to the Winning of Calais and Guisnes by the French in January, 1556.

4. The Coronation Procession of Queen ELIZABETH. January, 1559.

5. Sir THOMAS OVERBURY. Observations of Holland, Flanders, and France, in 1609. A most sagacious Political Study.

6. JAMES I. The Book of Sports. 1618

7. Abp. G. ABBOTT. Narrative of his Sequestration from Office in 1627 by CHARLES I., at the instigation of BUCKINGHAM and LAUD.

8. Major-General Sir T. MORGAN. Progress [*i.e. March*] in France and Flanders, with the 6,000 " Red Coats " at the taking of Dunkirk, etc., in 1657–8.

English Voyages, Travels, Commerce, etc., etc.

9. The first Britons who ever reached the city of Mexico: T. BLAKE, a Scotchman, before 1536; and J. FIELD and R. TOMSON, 1556.

10. The wonderful recovery of the *Exchange* from forty-five Turkish pirates of Algiers by J. RAWLINS and twenty-four other slaves. February, 1622.

English Life and Progress.

11. T. GENTLEMAN. England's Way to Win Wealth. [Fisheries.] The Dutch obtained more wealth from their Herring Fishery *along the English shores* than the Spaniards did from their American gold mines.

English Poetry.

12. ? T. OCCLEVE. The Letter of CUPID. 1402.

13. L. SHEPPARD. JOHN BON and Mast[er] PARSON. [A Satire on the Mass.] 1551.

14. Rev. T. BRICE. A Register of the Tormented and Cruelly Burned within England. 1555–1558. These verses give the names of most of the Marian Martyrs.

15. J. C. ALCILIA; PHILOPARTHEN's loving folly! [Love Poems.] 1595.

16. G. WITHER. Fair VIRTUE, the Mistress of PHIL'ARETE. 1622. This is WITHER's masterpiece. Over 6,000 lines of verse in many metrical forms.

17. The Songs that JOHN DOWLAND, the famous Lutenist, set to music.

VOL. V.

Large Crown 8vo, cloth, 5s. net.

English Political, Naval, and Military History, etc., etc.

1. J. SAVILE, King JAMES's entertainment at Theobalds, and his Welcome to London. 1603.
2. G. DUGDALE. The Time Triumphant. King JAMES's Coronation at Westminster, 25 July, 1603 ; and Coronation Procession [delayed by the Plague], 15 March, 1604.

English Voyages, Travels, Commerce, etc., etc.

3. The Voyages to Brazil of WILLIAM HAWKINS, Governor of Plymouth and father of Sir JOHN, about 1530.
4. Sir J. HAWKINS. First Voyage to the West Indies, 1562-1563. This was the beginning of the English Slave Trade.
5. R. BODENHAM. A Trip to Mexico. 1564-1565.
6. Sir J. HAWKINS. Second Voyage to the West Indies. 1564-1565.
7. Sir J. HAWKINS. Third and disastrous Voyage to the West Indies, 1567-1569 : with the base treachery of the Spaniards at San Juan de Ulna, near Vera Cruz; and the extraordinary adventures of Three of the Survivors. This was DRAKE's 2nd Voyage to the West Indies ; and the first in which he commanded a ship, the *Judith*.
8. Sir F. DRAKE's 3rd (1570), 4th (1571), and 5th (1572-73), Voyages to the West Indies. Especially the 5th, known as The Voyage to Nombre de Dios : in which, on 11 February, 1573, he first saw the Pacific Ocean ; and then besought GOD to give him life to sail once in an English ship on that sea. [See opposite page.]

English Life and Progress.

9. B. FRANKLIN. 'Poor Richard' improved. Proverbs of Thrift and to discourage useless expense. Philadelphia, 1757.

English Poetry.

10. B. BARNES. PARTHENOPHIL and PARTHENOPHE. Sonnets, Madrigals, Elegies and Odes. 1593. [A perfect Storehouse of Versification, including the only *treble* Sestine in the language.]
11. ZEPHERIA. [Canzons.] 1594.
12. Sir J. DAVIES. Orchestra or a Poem on Dancing. 1596.
13. B. GRIFFIN. FIDESSA, more chaste than kind. [Sonnets.] 1596.
14. Sir J. DAVIES. *Nosce teipsum!* In two Elegies : (1) Of Human Knowledge, (2) Of the Soul of Man and the Immortality thereof. 1599.
15. Sir J. Davies. Hymns of ASTRÆA [*i.e.* Queen ELIZABETH]. In acrostic verse. 1599.

VOL. VI.

Large Crown 8vo, cloth, 5s. net.

English Political, Naval, and Military History, etc., etc.

1. The Examination, at Saltwood Castle, Kent, of WILLIAM of THORPE, by Abp. T. ARUNDELL, 7 August, 1407. Edited by W. TYNDALE, 1530. This is the best account of Lollardism from the inside, given by one who was the leader of the second generation of Lollards.

English Voyages, Travels, Commerce, etc., etc.

2. J. CHILTON. Travels in Mexico. 1568–1575.
3. J. BION. An Account of the Torments, etc. 1708.

English Life and Progress.

4. The most dangerous Adventure of R. FERRIS, A. HILL, and W. THOMAS; who went in a boat by sea from London to Bristol. 1590.
5. Leather. A Discourse to Parliament. 1629.
6. H. PEACHAM. The Worth of a Penny, or a Caution to keep Money. 1641. With all the variations of the later Editions.
7. Sir W. PETTY. Political Arithmetic. [Written in 1677.] 1690. One of the earliest and best books on the Science of Wealth.

English Literature, Literary History, and Biography.

8. ISAAC BICKERSTAFF, Esq. [Dean J. Swift.] Predictions for the year 1708. [One of these was the death of J. PARTRIDGE, the *Almanack* Maker, on 29 March, 1708.] Other tracts of this laughable controversy follow.
9. [J. GAY.] The Present State of Wit. 3 May, 1711. [A Survey of our Periodical Literature at this date; including the *Review*, *Tatler*, and *Spectator*.]
10. [Dr. J. ARBUTHNOT.] Law [*i.e. War*] is a Bottomless Pit, exemplified in the Case of the Lord STRUTT [*the Kings of Spain*], JOHN BULL [*England*] the Clothier, NICHOLAS FROG [*Holland*] the Linendraper, and LEWIS BABOON [LOUIS XIV. of Bourbon= *France*]. In four parts. 1712.
This famous Political Satire on the War of the Spanish Succession was designed to prepare the English public for the Peace of Utrecht, signed on 11 April, 1713. In part I., on 28 February, 1712, first appeared in our Literature, the character of JOHN BULL, for an Englishman.
11. T. TICKELL. The life of ADDISON. 1721.
12. Sir R. STEELE. Epistle to W. CONGREVE [in reply]. 1722.

English Poetry.

13. The first printed *Robin Hood* Ballad. Printed about 1510.
14. W. PERCY. COELIA. [Sonnets.] 1594.
15. G. WITHER. FIDELIA. [This is WITHER's second master-

piece. The Lament of a Woman thinking that she is forsaken in love.] 1615.
16. M. DRAYTON. IDEA. [Sonnets.] 1619.
17. The Interpreter. [A Political Satire interpreting the meaning of the Protestant, The Puritan, The Papist.] 1622.

VOL. VII.

Large Crown 8vo, cloth, 5s. net.

English Political, Naval, and Military History, etc., etc.

1. Sir F. VERE, *General of the English troops in the Dutch service.* Commentaries of his Services : at (1) the Storming of Cadiz in 1596, (2) the Action at Turnhout in 1597, (3) The Battle of Nieuport in 1600 ; but especially (4) the Siege of Ostend, of which place he was Governor from 11 June, 1601, to 7 June, 1602.
2. The retaking of *The Friends' Adventure* from the French by R. LYDE and a boy. 1693.

English Voyages, Travels, Commerce, etc., etc.

3. H. PITMAN. Relation, etc. For doing noble Red Cross work at the Battle of Sedgemoor this surgeon was sent as a White Slave to Barbadoes, etc. 1689.

English Life and Progress.

4. W. KEMP'S [SHAKESPEARE'S fellow Actor] Nine Days' Wonder ; performed in a Morris Dance from London to Norwich. April, 1600.
5. A series of Texts on the indignities offered to the Established Clergy, and especially the Private Chaplains, in the Restoration Age, by the Royalist laity ; including
Dr. J. EACHARD'S witty 'Grounds of the Contempt of the Clergy and Religion.' 1670.

English Literature, Literary History and Biography.

6. Another Series of Tracts, in prose and verse, illustrating the great Public Services rendered by D. DEFOE, up to the death of Queen Anne ; including :
D. DEFOE. An Appeal to Honour and Justice, etc. 1715.
D. DEFOE. The *True* Born Englishman. 1701.
D. DEFOE. The History of *Kentish Petition.* 1701.
D. DEFOE. LEGION'S *Memorial.* 1701.
D. DEFOE. The Shortest Way with the Dissenters, etc. 1702.
D. DEFOE. A Hymn to the Pillory. 1703.
D. DEFOE. Prefaces to the *Review.* 1704-1710.

English Poetry.

7. T. DELONEY. Three Ballads on the Armada fight. August, 1588.
8. R. L. (1) DIELLA [Sonnets] ; (2) The Love of DOM DIEGO and GYNEURA. 1596.

English Reprints.

(For full titles, etc., see pp. 10-19.)

1. JOHN MILTON.
Areopagitica. 1644.

(a) AREOPAGITICA : *A Speech of Mr.* JOHN MILTON *For the Liberty of Unlicenc'd Printing, To the Parliament of England.*

(b) A Decree of Starre-Chamber, concerning Printing, made the eleuenth of July last past, 1637.

(c) An Order of the Lords and Commons assembled in Parliament for the Regulating of Printing, &c. 1643.

LORD MACAULAY. He attacked the licensing system in that sublime treatise which every statesman should wear as a sign upon his hand, and as frontlets between his eyes.—*Edinburgh Review, p.* 344, *August,* 1825.

H. HALLAM. Many passages in this famous tract are admirably eloquent : an intense love of liberty and truth flows through it ; the majestic soul of MILTON breathes such high thoughts as had not been uttered before. —*Introduction to the Literature of Europe,* iii. 660. *Ed.* 1839.

W. H. PRESCOTT. The most splendid argument perhaps the world had then witnessed on behalf of intellectual liberty.—*History of FERDINAND and ISABELLA,* iii. 391. *Ed.* 1845.

2. HUGH LATIMER.
Ex-Bishop of Worcester.
The Ploughers. 1549.

A notable Sermon of ye reuerende Father Master HUGHE LATIMER, *whiche he preached in ye Shrouds at paules churche in London on the xviii daye of Januarye.*

SIR R. MORISON. Did there ever any one (I say not in England only, but among other nations) flourish since the time of the Apostles, who preached the gospel more sincerely, purely, and honestly, than HUGH LATIMER, Bishop of *Worcester?*—*Apomaxis Calumniarum* . . *quibus JOANNES COCLEUS &c.,* f. 78. *Ed.* 1537.

It was in this Sermon, that LATIMER (himself an ex-Bishop) astonished his generation by saying that the Devil was the most diligent Prelate and Preacher in all England. " Ye shal neuer fynde him idle I warraunte you."

3. STEPHEN GOSSON.
Stud. Oxon.
The School of Abuse. 1579.

(a) *The Schoole of Abuse. Conteining a pleasaunt inuectiue against Poets, Pipers, Plaiers, Jesters, and such like Caterpillers of a Commonwealth ; Setting up the Flagge of Defiance to their mischieuous exercise and ouerthrowing their Bulwarkes, by Prophane Writers, Naturall reason and common experience.* 1579.

(b) *An Apologie of the Schoole of Abuse, against Poets, Pipers, Players, and their Excusers.* [*Dec.*] 1579.

∴ This attack is thought to have occasioned SIR PHILIP SIDNEY's writing of the following *Apologie for Poesie.*

GOSSON was, in succession, Poet, Actor, Dramatist, Satirist, and a Puritan Clergyman.

4. Sir PHILIP SIDNEY.

An Apology for Poetry.   [? 1580.]

An Apologie for Poetrie.   Written by the right noble, vertuous,
and learned Sir PHILIP SIDNEY, Knight.   1595.

H. W. LONGFELLOW.   The defence of Poetry is a work of rare merit. It
is a golden little volume, which the scholar may lay beneath his pillow, as
CHRYSOSTOM did the works of ARISTOPHANES.—*North American Review,*
p. 57.   January, 1832.

The Work thus divides itself :—

The Etymology of Poetry.
The Anatomy of the Effects of Poetry.
The Anatomy of the Parts of Poetry.
Objections to Poetry answered.
Criticism of the existing English Poetry.

5. EDWARD WEBBE,

A Chief Master Gunner.

Travels.   1590.

The rare and most wonderful thinges which EDWARD WEBBE
an Englishman borne, hath seene and passed in his troublesome
trauailes, in the Cities of Ierusalem, Damasko, Bethelem and
Galely : and in all the landes of Iewrie, Egipt, Grecia, Russia,
and in the Land of Prester John.

Wherein is set foorth his extreame slauerie sustained many
yeres togither, in the Gallies and wars of the great Turk against
the Landes of Persia, Tartaria, Spaine, and Portugall, with the
manner of his releasement and coming to England.   [1590.]

6. JOHN SELDEN.

Table Talk.   [1634-1654.]

Table Talk : being the Discourses of JOHN SELDEN, Esq. ; or
his Sence of various Matters of weight and high consequence,
relating especially to Religion and State.   1689.

S. T. COLERIDGE.   There is more weighty bullion sense in this book than
I ever found in the same number of pages of any uninspired writer. . . .
O ! to have been with SELDEN over his glass of wine, making every accident
an outlet and a vehicle of wisdom.—*Literary Remains,* iii. 361-2.   *Ed.*
1836.

H. HALLAM.   This very short and small volume gives, perhaps, a more
exalted notion of SELDEN's natural talents than any of his learned writings.
—*Introduction to the Literature of Europe,* iii. 347.   *Ed.* 1836.

Above all things, Liberty.

7. ROGER ASCHAM.

Toxophilus. 1544.

Toxophilus, the Schole of Shootinge, conteyned in two bookes.
To all Gentlemen and yomen of Englande, pleasaunte for theyr
pastime to rede, and profitable for theyr use to follow both in war
and peace.

In a dialogue between *TOXOPHILUS* and *PHILOLOGUS*, ASCHAM not
only gives us one of the very best books on Archery in our language : but
as he tells King Henry VIII., in his Dedication, "this litle treatise was
purposed, begon, and ended of me, onelie for this intent, that Labour,
Honest pastime, and Vertu might recouer againe that place and right, that
Idlenesse, Unthriftie Gaming, and Vice hath put them fro."

8. JOSEPH ADDISON.

Criticism on *Paradise Lost.* 1711-1712.

From the *Spectator*, being its Saturday issues between 31 December, 1711,
and 3 May, 1712. In these papers, which constitute a Primer to *Paradise
Lost*, ADDISON first made known, and interpreted to the general English
public, the great Epic poem, which had then been published nearly half a
century.

After a general discussion of the *Fable*, the *Characters*, the *Sentiments*,
the *Language*, and the *Defects* of MILTON's Great Poem ; the Critic devotes
a Paper to the consideration of the *Beauties* of each of its Twelve Books.

9. JOHN LYLY,

Novelist, Wit, Poet, and Dramatist.

Euphues. 1579-1580.

EUPHVES, *the Anatomy af Wit. Very pleasant for all
Gentlemen to reade, and most necessary to remember.*

*VVherein are conteined the delights that Wit followeth in his
youth, by the pleasantnesse of loue, and the happinesse he reapeth
in age by the perfectnesse of Wisedome.* 1579.

EUPHUES *and his England. Containing his voyage and
aduentures, myxed with sundry pretie discourses of honest Loue,
the description of the countrey, the Court, and the manners of
that Isle.* 1580.

Of great importance in our Literary History.

10. GEORGE VILLIERS,
Second Duke of BUCKINGHAM.
The Rehearsal. 1671.

The Rehearsal, as it was Acted at the Theatre Royal.

Many of the passages of anterior plays that were parodied in this famous Dramatic Satire on DRYDEN in the character of *BAYES*, are placed on opposite pages to the text. BRIAN FAIRFAX's remarkable life of this Duke of BUCKINGHAM is also prefixed to the play.

The Heroic Plays, first introduced by Sir W. D'AVENANT, and afterwards greatly developed by DRYDEN, are the object of this laughable attack. LACY, who acted the part of *BAYES*, imitated the dress and gesticulation of DRYDEN.

The Poet repaid this compliment to the Duke of BUCKINGHAM, in 1681, by introducing him in the character of *ZIMRA* in his *ABSOLOM and ACHITOPHEL.*

11. GEORGE GASCOIGNE,
Soldier and Poet.
The Steel Glass, &c. 1576.

(*a*) *A Remembrance of the wel imployed life, and godly end, of* GEORGE GASKOIGNE, *Esquire, who deceassed at Stalmford in Lincoln shire, the 7 of October,* 1577. *The reporte of* GEOR. WHETSTONS, *Gent.* 1577.

There is only one copy of this metrical Life. It is in the Bodleian Library.

(*b*) *Certayne notes of instruction concerning the making of verse or ryme in English.* 1575.

This is our First printed piece of Poetical Criticism.

(*c*) *The Steele Glas.*

Written in blank verse.

Probably the fourth printed English Satire : those by BARCLAY, ROY, and Sir T. WYATT being the three earlier ones.

(*d*) *The complaynt of* PHILOMENE. *An Elegie.* 1576.

12. JOHN EARLE,
Afterwards Bishop of SALISBURY.
Microcosmographie. 1628.

Micro-cosmographie, or a Peece of the World discovered ; in Essays and Characters.

This celebrated book of Characters is graphically descriptive of the English social life of the time, as it presented itself to a young Fellow of Merton College, Oxford ; including *A She precise Hypocrite, A Sceptic in Religion, A good old man,* etc.

This Work is a notable specimen of a considerable class of books in our Literature, full of interest : and which help Posterity much better to understand the Times in which they were written.

13. HUGH LATIMER,
Ex-Bishop of WORCESTER.

Seven Sermons before Edward VI. 1549.

The fyrste [—seuenth] Sermon of Mayster HUGHE LATIMER, *whiche he preached before the Kynges Maiestie wythin his graces palayce at Westminster on each Friday in Lent.* 1549.

Sir JAMES MACKINTOSH. LATIMER, . . . brave, sincere, honest, inflexible, not distinguished as a writer or a scholar, but exercising his power over men's minds by a fervid eloquence flowing from the deep conviction which animated his plain, pithy, and free-spoken Sermons.—*History of England*, ii. 291. *Ed.* 1831.

14. Sir THOMAS MORE.
Translation of Utopia. 1516-1557.

A frutefull and pleasaunt worke of the best state of a publique weale, and of the new yle called Utopia: VVritten in Latine by Sir THOMAS MORE, *Knyght, and translated into Englyshe by* RALPH ROBYNSON.

LORD CAMPBELL. Since the time of PLATO there had been no composition given to the world which, for imagination, for philosophical discrimination, for a familiarity with the principles of government, for a knowledge of the springs of human action, for a keen observation of men and manners, and for felicity of expression, could be compared to the *Utopia.*—*Lives of the Lord Chancellors (Life of Sir. T. More*), i. 583. *Ed.* 1845.

In the imaginary country of Utopia, MORE endeavours to sketch out a State based upon two principles—(1) community of goods, no private property; and consequently (2) no use for money.

15. GEORGE PUTTENHAM,
A Gentleman Pensioner to Queen ELIZABETH.

The Art of English Poesy. 1589.

· The Arte of English Poesie. Contriued into three Bookes: The first of POETS *and* POESIE, *the second of* PROPORTION, *the third of* ORNAMENT.

W. OLDYS. It contains many pretty observations, examples, characters, and fragments of poetry for those times, now nowhere else to be met with.— *Sir WALTER RALEIGH*, liv. *Ed.* 1736.

O. GILCHRIST. On many accounts one of the most curious and entertaining, and intrinsically one of the most valuable books of the age of QUEEN ELIZABETH. The copious intermixture of contemporary anecdote, tradition, manners, opinions, and the numerous specimens of coeval poetry nowhere else preserved, contribute to form a volume of infinite amusement, curiosity, and value.—*Censura Literaria*, i. 339. *Ed.* 1805.

This is still also an important book on Rhetoric and the Figures of Speech.

16. JAMES HOWELL,

Clerk of the Council to CHARLES I.; afterwards Historiographer to CHARLES II.

Instructions for Foreign Travel. 1642.

Instructions for forreine travelle. Shewing by what cours, and in what compasse of time, one may take an exact Survey of the Kingdomes and States of Christendome, and arrive to the practical knowledge of the Languages, to good purpose.

The *MURRAY, BÆDEKER,* and *Practical Guide* to the Grand Tour of Europe, which, at that time, was considered the finishing touch to the complete education of an English Gentleman.

The route sketched out by this delightfully quaint Writer, is France, Spain, Italy, Switzerland, Germany, the Netherlands, and Holland. The time allowed is 3 years and 4 months : the months to be spent in travelling, the years in residence at the different cities.

17. NICHOLAS UDALL,

Master, first of Eton College, then of Westminster School.

Roister Doister. [1553-1566.]

This is believed to be the first true English Comedy that ever came to the press.

From the unique copy, which wants a title-page, now at Eton College ; and which is thought to have been printed in 1566.

Dramatis Personæ.

RALPH ROISTER DOISTER.
MATTHEW MERRYGREEK.
GAWIN GOODLUCK, *affianced to Dame* CUSTANCE.
TRISTRAM TRUSTY, *his friend.*
DOBINET DOUGHTY, *" boy " to* ROISTER DOISTER.
TOM TRUEPENNY, *servant to Dame* CUSTANCE.
SIM SURESBY, *servant to* GOODLUCK.
Scrivener.
Harpax.
Dame CHRISTIAN CUSTANCE, *a widow.*
MARGERY MUMBLECRUST, *her nurse.*
TIBET TALKAPACE } *her maidens.*
ANNOT ALYFACE }

18. A Monk of Evesham,

The Revelation, &c. 1186[-1410]. 1485.

¶ *Here begynnyth a marvellous reuelacion that was schewyd of almighty god by sent Nycholas to a monke of Euyshamme yn the days of Kynge Richard the fyrst. And the yere of owre lord, M. C. Lxxxxvi.*

One of the rarest of English books printed by one of the earliest of English printers, WILLIAM DE MACLINIA ; who printed this text about 1485, *in the lifetime of CAXTON.*

The essence of the story is as old as it professes to be ; but contains later additions, the orthography, being of about 1410. It is very devoutly written, and contains a curious Vision of Purgatory.

The writer is a prototype of BUNYAN ; and his description of the Gate in the Crystal Wall of Heaven, and of the solemn and marvellously sweet Peal of the Bells of Heaven that came to him through it, is very beautiful.

19. JAMES I.

A Counterblast to Tobacco. 1604.

(a) The Essays of a Prentise, in the Diuine Art of Poesie.

Printed while JAMES VI. of Scotland, at Edinburgh in 1585; and includes *Ane Short treatise, conteining some Reulis and Cautelis to be obseruit and eschewit in Scottis Poesie,* which is another very early piece of printed Poetical Criticism.

(b) A Counterblaste to Tobacco. 1604.

To this text has been added a full account of *the Introduction and Early use of Tobacco in England.* The herb first came into use in Europe as a medicinal leaf for poultices: smoking it was afterwards learnt from the American Indians.

Our Royal Author thus sums up his opinion :—

"A custome lothsome to the eye, hateful to the nose, harmefull to the braine, dangerous to the lungs, and in the blacke stinking fume thereof, nearest resembling the horrible Stigian smoke of the pit that is bottomlesse."

20. Sir ROBERT NAUNTON,

Master of the Court of Wards.

Fragmenta Regalia. 1653.

Fragmenta Regalia: or Observations on the late Queen ELIZABETH, *her Times and Favourites.* [1630.]

Naunton writes :—

"And thus I have delivered up this my poor Essay; a little Draught of this great Princess, and her Times, with the Servants of her State and favour."

21. THOMAS WATSON,

Londoner, Student-at-Law.

Poems. 1582-1593.

(a) The Ἑκατομπαθια *or Passionate Centurie of Loue.*

Divided into two parts: whereof, the first expresseth the Author's sufferance in Loue: the latter, his long farwell to Loue and all his tyrannie. 1582.

(b) MELIBŒUS, *Sive Ecloga in obitum Honoratissimi Viri Domini* FRANCISCI WALSINGHAMI. 1590.

(c) The same translated into English, by the Author. 1590.

(d) The Tears of Fancie, or Loue disdained. 1593.

From the *unique* copy, wanting *Sonnets* 9-16, in the possession of S. CHRISTIE MILLER, Esq., of Britwell.

22. WILLIAM HABINGTON,

Castara. 1640.

CASTARA. *The third Edition. Corrected and augmented.*

CASTARA was Lady LUCY HERBERT, the youngest child of the first Lord POWIS; and these Poems were chiefly marks of affection during a pure courtship followed by a happy marriage. With these, are also Songs of Friendship, especially those referring to the Hon. GEORGE TALBOT.

In addition to these Poems, there are four prose Characters; on *A Mistress, A Wife, A Friend,* and *The Holy Man.*

23. ROGER ASCHAM,

The Schoolmaster. 1570.

The Scholemaster, or plane and perfite way of teachyng children to understand, write, and speake, in Latin tong, but specially purposed for the priuate brynging up of youth in Ientleman and Noble mens houses, &c.

This celebrated Work contains the story of Lady JANE GREY's delight in reading *PLATO,* an attack on the *Italianated* Englishman of the time, and much other information not specified in the above title.

In it, ASCHAM gives us very fully his plan of studying Languages, which may be described as *the double translation of a model book.*

24. HENRY HOWARD,

Earl of SURREY.

Sir THOMAS WYATT.

NICHOLAS GRIMALD.

Lord VAUX.

Tottel's Miscellany. 5 June, 1557.

Songes and Sonettes, vvritten by the right honourable Lorde HENRY HOWARD *late Earle of* SURREY, *and other.*

With 39 additional Poems from the second edition by the same printer, RICHARD TOTTEL, of 31 July, 1557.

This celebrated Collection is the First of our Poetical Miscellanies, and also the first appearance in print of any considerable number of English Sonnets.

TOTTEL in his *Address to the Reader,* says:—

"That to haue wel written in verse, yea and in small parcelles, deserueth great praise, the workes of diuers Latines, Italians, and other, doe proue sufficiently. That our tong is able in that kynde to do as praiseworthely as ye rest, the honorable stile of the noble earle of Surrey, and the weightinesse of the depewitted Sir Thomas Wyat the elders verse, with seuerall graces in sondry good Englishe writers, doe show abundantly."

25. Rev. THOMAS LEVER,
Fellow and Preacher of St. John's College, Cambridge.

Sermons. 1550.

(*a*) *A fruitfull Sermon in Paules church at London in the Shroudes.*

(*b*) *A Sermon preached the fourth Sunday in Lent before the Kynges Maiestie, and his honourable Counsell.*

(*c*) *A Sermon preached at Pauls Crosse.* 1550.

These Sermons are reprinted from the original editions, which are of *extreme* rarity. They throw much light on the communistic theories of the Norfolk rebels; and the one at Paul's Cross contains a curious account of Cambridge University life in the reign of EDWARD VI.

26. WILLIAM WEBBE,
Graduate.

A Discourse of English Poetry. 1586.

A Discourse of English Poetrie. Together with the Authors iudgement, touching the reformation of our English Verse.

Another of the early pieces of Poetical Criticism, written in the year in which SHAKESPEARE is supposed to have left Stratford for London.

Only two copies of this Work are known, one of these was sold for £64.

This Work should be read with STANYHURST's *Translation of Æneid, I.-IV.*, 1582, see p. 64. WEBBE was an advocate of English Hexameters; and here translates VIRGIL's first two Eglogues into them. He also translates into Sapphics COLIN's Song in the Fourth Eglogue of SPENSER's *Shepherd's Calendar.*

27. FRANCIS BACON.
afterwards Lord VERULAM Viscount ST. ALBANS.

A Harmony of the *Essays,* &c. 1597-1626.

*And after my manner, I alter ever, when I add. So that nothing is finished, till all be finished.—*Sir FRANCIS BACON, 27 Feb., 1610-[11].

(*a*) *Essays, Religious Meditations, and Places of perswasion and disswasion.* 1597.

(*b*) *The Writings of Sir* FRANCIS BACON *Knight the Kinges Sollicitor General in Moralitie, Policie, Historie.*

(*c*) *The Essaies of Sir* FRANCIS BACON *Knight, the Kings Solliciter Generall.*

(*d*) *The Essayes or Counsells, Civill and Morall of* FRANCIS *Lord* VERULAM, *Viscount* ST. ALBAN. 1625.

28. WILLIAM ROY. JEROME BARLOW.
Franciscan Friars.
Read me, and be not wroth! [1528.]

(*a*) *Rede me and be nott wrothe,*
For I saye no thynge but trothe.
I will ascende makynge my state so hye,
That my pompous honoure shall never dye.
O Caytyfe when thou thynkest least of all,
With confusion thou shalt have a fall.

This is the famous satire on Cardinal WOLSEY, and is the First English *Protestant* book ever printed, not being a portion of Holy Scripture. See *p.* 22 for the Fifth such book.

The next two pieces form one book, printed by HANS LUFT, at Marburg, in 1530.

(*b*) *A proper dyaloge, betwene a Gentillman and a husband-man, eche complaynynge to other their miserable calamite, through the ambicion of the clergye.*

(*c*) *A compendious old treatyse, shewynge, how that we ought to have the scripture in Englysshe.*

29. Sir WALTER RALEIGH. GERVASE MARKHAM. J. H. VAN LINSCHOTEN.
The Last Fight of the "Revenge." 1591.

(*a*) *A Report of the truth of the fight about the Iles of Acores, this last la Sommer. Betwixt the* REUENGE, *one of her Maiesties Shippes, and an* ARMADA *of the King of Spaine.*
[By Sir W. RALEIGH.]

(*b*) *The most honorable Tragedie of Sir* RICHARD GRINUILE, *Knight.* 1595.
[By GERVASE MARKHAM.]

(*c*) [*The Fight and Cyclone at the Azores.*
[By JAV HUYGHEN VAN LINSCHOTEN.]

Several accounts are here given of one of the most extraordinary Sea fights in our Naval History.

30. BARNABE GOOGE.
Eglogues, Epitaphs, and Sonnets. 1563.

Eglogs, Epytaphes, and Sonettes Newly written by BARNABE GOOGE.

Three copies only known. Reprinted from the *Huth* copy.

In the prefatory *Notes of the Life and Writings of B. GOOGE,* will be found an account of the trouble he had in winning MARY DARELL for his wife.

A new Literature generally begins with imitations and translations. When this book first appeared, Translations were all the rage among the "young England" of the day. This Collection of *original* Occasional Verse is therefore the more noticeable. The Introduction gives a glimpse of the principal Writers of the time, such as the Authors of the *Mirror for Magistrates*, the Translators of SENECA'S *Tragedies*, etc., and including such names as BALDWIN, BAVANDE, BLUNDESTON, NEVILLE, NORTH, NORTON, SACKVILLE, and YELVERTON.

The English Scholar's Library.

16 Parts are now published, in Cloth Boards, £2 1s.
Any part may be obtained separately.
The general character of this Series will be gathered
from the following pages :—21-26.

		s.	*d.*
1. WILLIAM CAXTON. **Reynard the Fox.**		1	6
2. JOHN KNOX. **The First Blast of the Trumpet**		1	6
3. CLEMENT ROBINSON and *others*. **A handful of Pleasant Delights**		1	6
4. [SIMON FISH.] **A Supplication for the Beggars**		1	6
5. [*Rev*. JOHN UDALL.] **Diotrephes.**		1	6
6. [?] **The Return from Parnassus**		1	6
7. THOMAS DECKER. **The Seven Deadly Sins of London**		1	6
8. EDWARD ARBER. **An Introductory Sketch to the " Martin Marprelate " Controversy, 1588-1590**		3	0
9. [*Rev*. JOHN UDALL.] **A Demonstration of Discipline**		1	6
10. RICHARD STANIHURST. **" Æneid I.-IV."** in English hexameters.		3	0
11. **" The Epistle "**		1	6
12. ROBERT GREEN. **Menaphon**		1	6
13. GEORGE JOY. **An Apology to William Tyndale**		1	6
14. RICHARD BARNFIELD. **Poems**		3	0
15. *Bp*. THOMAS COOPER. **An Admonition to the People of England**		3	0
16. *Captain* JOHN SMITH. **Works.** 1120 pages. Six Facsimile Maps. 2 Vols		12	6

1. William Caxton,
our first Printer.
Translation of REYNARD THE FOX. 1481.

[COLOPHON.] *I haue not added ne mynusshed but haue folowed as nyghe as I can my copye which was in dutche | and by me* WILLIAM CAXTON *translated in to this rude and symple englyssh in th[e] abbey of westmestre.*

Interesting for its own sake; but especially as being translated as well as printed by CAXTON, who finished the printing on 6 June, 1481.

The Story is the History of the Three fraudulent Escapes of the Fox from punishment, the record of the Defeat of Justice by flattering lips and dishonourable deeds. It also shows the struggle between the power of Words and the power of Blows, a conflict between Mind and Matter. It was necessary for the physically weak to have Eloquence : the blame of REYNARD is in the frightful misuse he makes of it.

The author says, "There is in the world much seed left of the Fox, wh'.h now over all groweth and cometh sore up, though they have no red beards."

2. John Knox,
the Scotch Reformer.
THE FIRST BLAST OF THE TRUMPET, &C.
1558.

(*a*) *The First Blast of a Trumpet against the monstrous Regiment of Women.*

(*b*) *The Propositions to be entreated in the Second* BLAST.

This work was wrung out of the heart of JOHN KNOX, while, at Dieppe, he heard of the martyr fires of England, and was anguished thereby. At that moment the liberties of Great Britain, and therein the hopes of the whole World, lay in the laps of four women—MARY of Loraine, the Regent of Scotland ; her daughter MARY (the Queen of Scots); Queen MARY TUDOR ; and the Princess ELIZABETH.

The Volume was printed at Geneva.

(*c*) KNOX'S *apologetical Defence of his* FIRST BLAST; &c., *to Queen* ELIZABETH. 1559.

3. Clement Robinson,
and divers others.
A HANDFUL OF PLEASANT DELIGHTS.
1584.

A Handeful of pleasant delites, Containing sundrie new Sonets and delectable Histories, in diuers kindes of Meeter. Newly deuised to the newest tunes that are now in vse, to be sung : euerie Sonet orderly pointed to his proper Tune. With new additions of certain Songs, to verie late deuised Notes, not commonly knowen, nor vsed heretofore.

OPHELIA quotes from *A Nosegaie, &c.*, in this Poetical Miscellany ; of which only one copy is now known.

It also contains the earliest text extant of the *Ladie Greensleeues*, which first appeared four years previously.

This is the Third printed Poetical Miscellany in our language.

4. [Simon Fish,
of Gray's Inn.]

A SUPPLICATION FOR THE BEGGARS.
[? 1529.]

A Supplicacyon for the Beggars.

Stated by J. Fox to have been distributed in the streets of London on Candlemas Day [2 Feb., 1529].
This is the Fifth Protestant book (not being a portion of Holy Scripture that was printed in the English Language.
The authorship of this anonymous tract, is fixed by a passage in Sir T. MORE's *Apology*, of 1533, quoted in the Introduction.

5. [Rev. John Udall,
Minister at Kingston on Thames.]

DIOTREPHES. [1588.]

The state of the Church of Englande, laid open in a conference betweene DIOTREPHES *a Byshopp,* TERTULLUS *a Papiste,* DEMETRIUS *an vsurer,* PANDOCHUS *an Innekeeper, and* PAULE *a preacher of the word of God.*

This is the forerunning tract of the *MARTIN MARPRELATE Controversy.* For the production of it, ROBERT WALDEGRAVE, the printer, was ruined ; and so became available for the printing of the Martinist invectives.
The scene of the Dialogue is in PANDOCHUS'S Inn, which is in a posting-town on the high road from London to Edinburgh.

6. [?   ]

THE RETURN FROM PARNASSUS.
[Acted 1602.]   1606.

The Returne from Pernassus : or The Scourge of Simony. Publiquely acted by the Students in Saint Iohns Colledge in Cambridge.

This play, written by a University man in December, 1601, brings WILLIAM KEMP and RICHARD BURBAGE on to the Stage, and makes them speak thus :
" KEMP.   Few of the vniuersity pen plaies well, they smell too much of that writer *Ouid* and that writer *Metamorphosis,* and talke too much of *Proserpina* and *Iuppiter.* Why heeres our fellow *Shakespeare* puts them all downe, I [*Ay*] and *Ben Ionson* too. O that *Ben Ionson* is a pestilent fellow, he brought vp *Horace* giuing the Poets a pill, but our fellow *Shakespeare* hath given him a purge that made him beray his credit :
" BURBAGE.   It's a shrewd fellow indeed : "
What this controversy between SHAKESPEARE and JONSON was, has not yet been cleared up. It was evidently recent, when (in Dec., 1601) this play was written.

7. Thomas Decker,
The Dramatist.
THE SEVEN DEADLY SINS OF LONDON, &C. 1606.

The seuen deadly Sinnes of London : drawn in seuen seuerall Coaches, through the seuen seuerall Gates of the Citie, bringing the Plague with them.

A prose Allegorical Satire, giving a most vivid picture of London life, in October, 1606.

The seven sins are—

> FRAUDULENT BANKRUPTCY.
> LYING.
> CANDLELIGHT (*Deeds of Darkness*).
> SLOTH.
> APISHNESS (*Changes of Fashion*).
> SHAVING (*Cheating*), and CRUELTY.

Their chariots, drivers, pages, attendants, and followers, are all allegorically described.

8. *The Editor.*
AN INTRODUCTORY SKETCH TO THE MARTIN MARPRELATE CONTROVERSY.
1588–1590.

(*a*) *The general Episcopal Administration, Censorship, &c.*
(*b*) *The Origin of the Controversy.*
(*c*) *Depositions and Examinations.*
(*d*) *State Documents.*
(*e*) *The Brief held by Sir* JOHN PUCKERING, *against the Martinists.*

The REV. J. UDALL (who was, however, *not* a Martinist) ; Mrs. CRANE, of Molesey, Rev. J. PENRY, Sir R. KNIGHTLEY, of Fawsley, near Northampton ; HUMPHREY NEWMAN, the London cobbler ; JOHN HALES, Esq., of Coventry ; Mr. and Mrs. WEEKSTON, of Wolston : JOB THROCKMORTON, Esq.; HENRY SHARPE, bookbinder of Northampton, and the four printers.

(*f*) *Miscellaneous Information.*
(*g*) *Who were the Writers who wrote under the name of* MARTIN MARPRELATE?

9. [Rev. John Udall,
Minister at Kingston on Thames.]
A DEMONSTRATION OF DISCIPLINE. 1588.

A Demonstration of the trueth of that discipline which CHRISTE *hath prescribed in his worde for the gouernement of his Church, in all times and places, vntil the ende of the worlde.*

Printed with the secret Martinist press, at East Molesey, near Hampton Court, in July, 1588 ; and secretly distributed with the *Epitome* in the following November.

For this Work, UDALL lingered to death in prison.

It is perhaps the most complete argument, in our language, for Presbyterian Puritanism, as it was then understood. Its author asserted for it, the infallibility of a Divine Logic ; but two generations had not passed away, before (under the teachings of Experience) much of this Church Polity had been discarded.

10. Richard Stanyhurst,
the Irish Historian.
Translation of ÆNEID I.–IV. 1582.

Thee first foure Bookes of VIRGIL *his Æneis translated intoo English heroical* [*i.e.*, hexameter] *verse by* RICHARD STANY-HURST, *wyth oother Poëtical diuises theretoo annexed.*
Imprinted at Leiden in Holland by IOHN PATES, *Anno M.D.LXXXII.*

This is one of the oddest and most grotesque books in the English language ; and having been printed in Flanders, the original Edition is of *extreme* rarity.
The present text is, by the kindness of Lord ASHBURNHAM and S. CHRISTIE-MILLER, Esq., reprinted from the only two copies known, neither of which is quite perfect.
GABRIRL HARVEY desired to be epitaphed, *The Inventor of the English Hexameter* ; and STANYHURST, in imitating him, went further than any one else in maltreating English words to suit the exigencies of Classical feet.

11. *Martin Marprelate.*
THE EPISTLE. 1588.

Oh read ouer D. JOHN BRIDGES, *for it is a worthy worke : Or an epitome of the fyrste Booke of that right worshipfull volume, written against the Puritanes, in the defence of the noble cleargie, by as worshipfull a prieste,* JOHN BRIDGES, *Presbyter, Priest or Elder, doctor of Diuillitie, and Deane of Sarum.*
The Epitome [*p.* 26] *is not yet published, but it shall be, when the Byshops are at convenient leysure to view the same. In the meane time, let them be content with this learned Epistle.*
Printed oversea, in Europe, within two furlongs of a Bounsing Priest, at the cost and charges of M. MARPRELATE, *gentleman.*

12. Robert Greene, M.A.
MENAPHON. 1589.

MENAPHON. CAMILLAS *alarum to slumbering* EUPHUES, *in his melancholie Cell at Silexedra. VVherein are deciphered the variable effects of Fortune, the wonders of Loue, the triumphes of inconstant Time. Displaying in sundrie conceipted passions (figured in a continuate Historie) the Trophees that Vertue carrieth triumphant, maugre the wrath of Enuie, or the resolution of Fortune.*

One of GREENE's novels with TOM NASH's Preface, so important in reference to the earlier *HAMLET*, before SHAKESPEARE's tragedy.
GREENE's "love pamphlets" were the most popular Works of Fiction in England, up to the appearance of Sir P. SIDNEY'S *Arcadia* in 1590.

13. George Joy,
an early Protestant Reformer.

AN APOLOGY TO TINDALE. 1535.

An Apologye made by GEORGE JOYE *to satisfye (if it may be)* W. TINDALE : *to pourge and defende himself ageinst so many sclaunderouse lyes fayned vpon him in* TINDAL'S *vncharitable and vnsober* Pystle *so well worthye to be prefixed* for the Reader *to induce him into the understanding of hys* new Testament diligently corrected and printed in the yeare of our Lorde, 1534, in Nouember [Antwerp, 27 Feb., 1535.

This almost lost book is our only authority in respect to the surreptitious editions of the English *New Testament*, which were printed for the English market with very many errors, by Antwerp printers who knew not English, in the interval between TINDALE'S first editions in 1526, and his revised Text (above referred to) in 1534.

14. Richard Barnfield.
of Darlaston, Staffordshire.

POEMS. 1594-1598.

The affectionate Shepherd. Containing the Complaint of DAPHNIS *for the Loue of* GANYMEDE.

In the following Work, BARNFIELD states that this is "an imitation of *Virgill*, in the second Eglogue of *Alexis*."

CYNTHIA. *With Certaine Sonnets, and the Legend of* CASSANDRA. 1595.

The Author thus concludes his Preface : "Thus, hoping you will beare with my rude conceit of *Cynthia* (if for no other cause, yet, for that it is the First Imitation of the verse of that excellent Poet, Maister *Spencer*, in his *Fayrie Queene*), I leaue you to the reading of that, which I so much desire may breed your delight."

The Encomion of Lady PECUNIA : *or, The Praise of Money.* 1598.

Two of the Poems in this Text have been wrongly attributed to SHAKESPEARE. The disproof is given in the Introduction.

15. T[homas] C[ooper].
[Bishop of WINCHESTER.]

ADMONITION TO THE PEOPLE OF ENGLAND.

An admonition to the people of England · VVherein are answvered, not onley the slaunderous vntruethes, reprochfully vttered by MARTIN *the Libeller, but also many other Crimes by some of his broode, objected generally against all Bishops, and the chiefe of the Cleargie, purposely to deface and discredit the present state of the Church.* [*Jan.* 1589].

This is the official reply on the part of the Hierarchy, to *MARTIN MARPRELATE's Epistle of* [Nov.] 1508 : see No. 11. on *p.* 24.

It was published between the appearance of the *Epistle* and that of the *Epitome*.

16.　Captain John Smith,

President of Virginia, and Admiral of New England.
WORKS.—1608-1631. 2 *vols.* 12*s.* 6*d.*
A complete edition, with six facsimile plates.

Occasion was taken, in the preparation of this Edition, dispassionately to test the Author's statements. The result is perfectly satisfactory. The Lincolnshire Captain is to be implicitly believed in all that he relates of his own personal knowledge.

The following are the chief Texts in this Volume :—
   (1.) **A true Relation of Occurrences in Virginia.** 1608.
   (2.) **A Map of Virginia.** 1612.
   (3.) **A Description of New England.** 1616.
   (4.) **New England's Trials.** 1620 and 1622.
   (5.) **The History of Virginia, New England, and Bermuda.** 1624.
   (6.) **An Accidence for young Seamen.** 1626.
   (7.) **His true Travels, Adventures, and Observations.** 1630.
   (8.) **Advertisements for Planters in New England, or anywhere.** 1631.

The first Three English Books on America.　[? 1511]–1555.

This work is a perfect Encyclopædia respecting the earliest Spanish and English Voyages to America.

Small Paper Edition, 456 *pp., in One Volume, Demy* 4*to,* £1 1*s.*

Large Paper Edition in One Volume, Royal 4*to,* £3 3*s.*

The Three Books are—
   (1.) **Of the new landes, etc.**　Printed at Antwerp about 1511. *This is the first English book in which the word* America [*i.e.* Armonica] *occurs.*
   (2.) **A Treatise of the new India, etc.**　Translated by RICHARD EDEN from SEBASTIAN MUENSTER'S *Cosmography:* and printed in 1553. *The Second English Book on America.*
   (3.) **The Decades of the New World, etc.**, by PIETRO MARTIRE [PETRUS MARTYR], translated by RICHARD EDEN, and printed in 1555. *The Third English Book on America.* SHAKESPEARE obtained the character of CALIBAN from this Work.

A List of 837 London Publishers,
1553–1640.

This Master Key to English Bibliography for the period also gives the approximate period that each Publisher was in business.

Demy 4*to,* 32 *pp.,* 10*s.* 6*d. net.*

Fcap. 4to, Cloth, Gilt, 10s. 6d. *net.*

THE ONLY KNOWN FRAGMENT OF

The First printed
English New Testament, in Quarto.

BY W. TINDALE AND W. ROY.

Sixty photo-lithographed pages ; preceded by a critical PREFACE.

BRIEFLY told, the story of this profoundly interesting work is as follows :—

In 1524 TINDALE went from London to Hamburgh ; where remaining for about a year, he journeyed on to Cologne ; and there, assisted by WILLIAM ROY, subsequently the author of the satire on WOLSEY, *Rede me and be nott wrothe* [see *p.* 19], he began this first edition in 4to, *with glosses*, of the English New Testament.

A virulent enemy of the Reformation, COCHLÆUS, at that time an exile in Cologne, learnt, through giving wine to the printer's men, that P. QUENTAL the printer had in hand a secret edition of three thousand copies of the English New Testament. In great alarm, he informed HERMAN RINCK, a Senator of the city, who moved the Senate to stop the printing ; but COCHLÆUS could neither obtain a sight of the Translators, nor a sheet of the impression.

TINDALE and ROY fled with the printed sheets up the Rhine to Worms ; and there completing this edition, produced also another in 8vo, *without glosses.* Both editions were probably in England by March, 1526.

Of the six thousand copies of which they together were composed, there remain but this fragment of the First commenced edition, in 4to ; and of the Second Edition, in 8vo, one complete copy in the Library of the Baptist College at Bristol, and an imperfect one in that of St. Paul's Cathedral, London.

In the *Preface,* the original documents are given intact, in connection with

Evidence connected with the first Two Editions of the English New Testament, viz., in Quarto and Octavo—

I.   WILLIAM TINDALE'S antecedent career.
II.   The Printing at Cologne.
III.   The Printing at Worms.
IV.   WILLIAM ROY'S connection with these Editions.
V.   The landing and distribution in England.
VI.   The persecution in England.

Typographical and Literary Evidence connected with the present Fragment—

I,   It was printed for TINDALE by PETER QUENTAL at Cologne, before 1526.
II.   It is not a portion of the separate Gospel of *Matthew* printed previous to that year.
III.   It is therefore certainly a fragment of the Quarto.

Is the Quarto a translation of LUTHER'S *German Version ?*

Text. The prologge. Inner Marginal References. Outer Marginal Glosses.

** For a continuation of this Story see G. JOY'S *Apology* at *p.* 25.

Captain **WILLIAM SIBORNE.**

The Waterloo Campaign. 1815.

4th Ed.   Crown 8vo.   832 *pages.*   13 *Medallion Portraits of Generals.*   15 *Maps and Plans.*

Bound in Red Cloth, uncut edges.   FIVE SHILLINGS, Net.

The Work is universally regarded to be the best general Account in the English language of the Twenty Days' War : including the Battles of Quatre Bras, Ligny, Waterloo, and Wavre ; and the subsequent daring March on Paris.   It is as fair to the French as it is to the Allies.

WILLIAM BEATTY, M.D., Surgeon of H.M.S. Victory.

An Authentic Narrative of the Death of Lord Nelson.

21st October, 1805.

2nd Ed.   Crown 8vo.   96 *pages.*   *Two Illustrations :*

(1) Of Lord **NELSON** in the dress he wore when he received his mortal wound.

(2) Of the Bullet that killed him.

Bound in Blue Cloth, uncut edges.   HALF-A-CROWN, Net.

The Paston Letters.

1422–1509.

A NEW EDITION, containing upwards of 400 letters, etc., hitherto unpublished.

EDITED BY

JAMES GAIRDNER,

Of the Public Record Office.

3 *Vols. Fcap. 8vo, Cloth extra,* 15s. *net.*

" *The Paston Letters* are an important testimony to the progressive condition of Society, and come in as a precious link in the chain of moral history of England, which they alone in this period supply. They stand, indeed, singly, as far as I know, in Europe ; for though it is highly probable that in the archives of Italian families, if not in France or Germany, a series of merely private letters equally ancient may be concealed ; I do not recollect that any have been published. They are all written in the reigns of HENRV VI. and EDWARD IV., except a few that extend as far as HENRV VII., by different members of a wealthy and respectable, but not noble, family; and are, therefore, pictures of the life of the English gentry of that age."— HENRV HALLAM, *Introduction to the Literature of Europe,* i. 228, *Ed.* 1837.

These Letters are the genuine correspondence of a family in Norfolk during the Wars of the Roses. As such, they are altogether unique in character ; yet the language is not so antiquated as to present any serious difficulty to the modern reader. The topics of the letters relate partly to the private affairs of the family, and partly to the stirring events of the time : and the correspondence includes State papers, love letters, bailiff's accounts, sentimental poems, jocular epistles, etc.

Besides the public news of the day, such as the Loss of Normandy by the English ; the indictment, and subsequent murder at sea of the Duke of SUFFOLK ; and all the fluctuations of the great struggle of YORK and LANCASTER ; we have the story of JOHN PASTON'S first introduction to his wife ; incidental notices of severe domestic discipline, in which his sister frequently had her head broken ; letters from Dame ELIZABETH BREWS, a match-making Mamma, who reminds the youngest JOHN PASTON that Friday is "Saint Valentine's Day," and invites him to come and visit her family from the Thursday evening till the Monday, etc., etc.

Every Letter has been exhaustively annotated ; and a Chronological Table, with most copious Indices, conclude the Work.

THE "WHITEHALL EDITION" OF THE WORKS OF WILLIAM SHAKESPEARE.

Edited from the Original Texts by H. ARTHUR DOUBLEDAY, with the assistance of T. GREGORY FOSTER and ROBERT ELSON.

In 12 volumes, imperial 16mo.

The special features to which the publishers would call attention are the TYPE, which is large enough to be read with comfort by all; the NUMBERING of the LINES, for convenience of reference; the ARRANGEMENT of the PLAYS in chronological order; and the GLOSSARY which is given at the end of each play. The text has been carefully edited from the original editions, and follows as nearly as possible that of the Folio of 1623. A few notes recording the emendations of modern Editors which have been adopted are printed at the end of each play.

The volumes are handsomely bound in buckram and in cloth, 5s. per volume. Also in half-parchment, gilt top, 6s. per volume.

SOME PRESS OPINIONS OF "THE WHITEHALL SHAKESPEARE."

" The print is clear, the paper good, the margin sufficient, and the volume not too cumbersome."—*Times*.

" The text gives every evidence of being edited with care and scholarship. . . . On the whole, *The Whitehall Shakespeare* promises to be one of the most generally attractive among the many editions of the bard which compete for public favour."—*Scotsman*.

" The general effect is excellent . . . it deserves a great success."—*National Observer*.

" *The Whitehall Shakespeare* commends itself by its convenient form, and its clear and handsome type, as well as by some special features, among which is the alphabetical index to all the characters in the plays in each volume."—*Daily News*.

" It combines, as far as possible, the requirements of a library and popular edition."—*Literary World*.

" There is certainly no edition of Shakespeare in the market which is more prettily got up or better printed. . . . One of the best editions for the general reader that have ever appeared in this country."—*Scottish Leader*.

" Paper, print, and binding leave little to be desired."—*Standard*.

WESTMINSTER : ARCHIBALD CONSTABLE & CO.,
14, PARLIAMENT STREET.

CPSIA information can be obtained
at www.ICGtesting.com
Printed in the USA
BVHW031459260819
556814BV00010B/1885/P